The Middle East Economy

A Rising Star

Unveiling the Middle East's Economic
& Investment Landscape

Bahaa G. Arnouk

ISBN: 978-1-0685581-9-1

Previously published as: "The Middle East In The Eyes Of The IMF" by Bahaa Arnouk

Book Cover by Bahaa Arnouk

2nd edition 2024

Bahaa G. Arnouk

Table of contents

Introduction

The Middle East, a region steeped in history and rich in resources, stands at a pivotal juncture in its economic evolution. As global dynamics shift and the world transitions towards a more sustainable future, the economies of the Middle East are navigating a complex landscape of challenges and opportunities. This book delves into the economic narratives of key Middle Eastern countries, drawing insights from unique and authoritative sources such as the International Monetary Fund (IMF) reports.

This book provides a nuanced and comprehensive analysis of the economic realities facing each nation and offers a valuable lens through which to understand the complexities of these economies, their strengths, vulnerabilities, and the policy choices shaping their trajectories.

From the oil-rich Gulf states to the emerging economies of the Levant, this book explores a diverse range of economic models, each facing its own set of challenges and opportunities. We will delve into the ongoing diversification efforts of countries like Saudi Arabia, Qatar, and Oman, as they seek to reduce their reliance on hydrocarbons and build more resilient and sustainable economies. We will examine the fiscal consolidation strategies of Kuwait and Egypt, as they grapple with high public debt and navigate the complexities of balancing debt reduction with essential social spending. We will analyse the structural reforms being implemented in Turkey and Jordan, as they strive to enhance competitiveness, attract investment, and create jobs for their growing populations. And we will explore the resilience and transformation of Cyprus, as it leverages its EU membership and strategic location to diversify its economy and position itself as a hub for innovation and investment.

This book excluded few economies where tension has escalated recently like Israel, Iran, Palestine, Lebanon Syria, and Yemen.

This book is not merely a collection of economic data and policy prescriptions; it is a narrative of transformation, resilience, and opportunity. Through this book, you will gain a deeper understanding of the forces shaping the economic destinies of these nations, the challenges they face, the choices they make, and the potential they hold. This book is an invitation to explore the Middle East's economic landscape, to understand its complexities, and to appreciate the remarkable journeys these countries are undertaking as they navigate the currents of global change.

Saudi Arabia - A Land of Opportunity Beyond Oil

Imagine a place where the whispers of ancient history mingle with the hum of futuristic innovation. That's Saudi Arabia today, a Kingdom in the midst of a dramatic transformation driven by the audacious vision of 2030. The latest IMF report paints a picture of this evolving landscape, revealing a nation balancing ambitious goals with a burgeoning array of opportunities. From giga-projects rising from the desert sands to a tech scene that rivals Silicon Valley, Saudi Arabia is captivating investors seeking growth and diversification. But this journey is not without its complexities. Join me as we delve into Saudi Arabia economic and investment landscape uncovering both the dazzling potential and the nuances that demand a discerning eye.

Saudi Arabia's economic transformation under Vision 2030 is creating a dynamic landscape brimming with opportunities for discerning investors. This chapter leverages amongst different sources, insights from the International Monetary Fund's (IMF) September 2024 Article IV Consultation report to provide an overview of the challenges and opportunities in the Saudi market.

Beyond Oil: A Deep Dive into Saudi Arabia's Diversification Success Story

While oil has long been the bedrock of Saudi Arabia's economy, the Kingdom is making impressive strides in diversifying its economic base. This shift, a cornerstone of the ambitious Vision

2030 plan, is bearing fruit, as evidenced by the robust performance of the non-oil sector. In FY2023, non-oil GDP growth reached a remarkable 3.8%, a testament to the Kingdom's commitment to fostering a vibrant and multifaceted economy.

This momentum is fuelled by a confluence of factors, with private consumption, non-oil investment, and a booming tourism sector playing pivotal roles. Let's delve deeper into each of these drivers:

Private Consumption: A Reflection of Economic Confidence

The strength of private consumption reflects growing consumer confidence in the Saudi economy. This confidence is underpinned by several factors, including:

Job Creation: Saudi Arabia's labor market has witnessed significant job creation, particularly in the private sector. This has resulted in a decline in unemployment, boosting disposable incomes and fuelling consumer spending.

Government Reforms: Fiscal reforms and improvements to the regulatory business environment have created a more conducive environment for private sector activity, leading to increased investment and job creation.

Social Programs: Targeted social programs, such as the Citizen Account Program, have provided a safety net for vulnerable households, supporting consumption, and mitigating the impact of economic fluctuations.

Non-Oil Investment: Laying the Foundation for Future Growth

Non-oil investment is another key driver of Saudi Arabia's diversification success. The Kingdom is making significant investments in infrastructure, technology, and human capital, laying the foundation for sustained economic growth in the years to come. Key areas of investment include:

Infrastructure Development: Mega-projects like NEOM, Roshn, and the Red Sea Global are driving massive investments in infrastructure, creating new cities, housing developments, and tourism destinations. These projects are attracting international businesses and creating new jobs, further fuelling economic growth.

Technology and Innovation: Saudi Arabia is investing heavily in technology and innovation, aiming to become a regional hub for technology and entrepreneurship. This includes investments in artificial intelligence, cloud computing, and cybersecurity, as well as initiatives to foster a vibrant startup ecosystem.

Human Capital Development: Recognizing the importance of a skilled workforce, Saudi Arabia is investing in education and training programs to equip its citizens with the skills needed for the jobs of the future. This includes initiatives to promote STEM education, vocational training, and entrepreneurship.

Tourism: A Rising Star in the Saudi Economy

Saudi Arabia's tourism sector is experiencing a remarkable boom, fuelled by a combination of factors, including:

Easing of Visa Restrictions: The introduction of tourist e-visas has made it easier for international travellers to visit Saudi Arabia, boosting tourism inflows.

Development of New Destinations: Mega-projects like the Red Sea Global and Qiddiya are creating world-class tourism destinations, attracting visitors from around the globe.

Promotion of Cultural Heritage: Saudi Arabia is promoting its rich cultural heritage, showcasing its ancient cities, historical sites, and traditional arts and crafts. This is attracting cultural tourists and diversifying the tourism sector beyond religious tourism.

The tourism sector's contribution to GDP: reached an impressive 11.5% in 2023, and the IMF projects further growth in the years to come. This growth is creating new jobs, boosting service sector activity, and contributing to the diversification of the Saudi economy.

The IMF's Outlook: Continued Non-Oil Growth: continued non-oil growth in the 3.9-4.4% range over the medium term is anticipated, driven by the ambitious National Investment Strategy (NIS) and the ongoing implementation of mega-projects. The report highlights the importance of maintaining the reform momentum, particularly in terms of fiscal consolidation and structural reforms, to ensure sustainable and inclusive growth.

Saudi Arabia's diversification journey is well underway, with the non-oil sector demonstrating remarkable resilience and growth potential. The Kingdom's commitment to investing in infrastructure, technology, human capital, and tourism is laying the foundation for a vibrant and diversified economy that is less reliant on oil.

Giga-Projects: Fuelling Saudi Arabia's Ambitious Transformation

Saudi Arabia's commitment to large-scale, transformative projects, known as "giga-projects," is a defining characteristic of its Vision 2030 plan. These ambitious endeavours, spearheaded by the Public Investment Fund (PIF) with its vast assets exceeding $925 billion, are reshaping the Kingdom's landscape, creating a multi-billion-dollar opportunity for international businesses across a spectrum of sectors.

These giga-projects are not merely about constructing impressive structures; they are about building entire ecosystems designed to diversify the economy, attract foreign investment, create jobs, and enhance the quality of life for Saudi citizens. Let's explore some of the most prominent giga-projects and the vast opportunities they unlock:

NEOM: A Beacon of Innovation and Technology

NEOM, a $500 billion futuristic mega-city envisioned as a global hub for innovation and technology, is perhaps the most ambitious of Saudi Arabia's giga-projects. Spanning 26,500 square kilometres, NEOM is designed to be a living laboratory for cutting-edge technologies, sustainable living, and advanced industries.

Opportunities for Businesses: NEOM presents a vast array of opportunities for businesses in sectors such as:

Construction and Engineering: The construction of NEOM requires expertise in a wide range of disciplines, from infrastructure development to sustainable building practices.

Technology and Innovation: NEOM is a hotbed for technological innovation, with opportunities for companies specializing in artificial intelligence, robotics, renewable energy, and smart city solutions.

Logistics and Transportation: NEOM's strategic location and advanced transportation systems create opportunities for logistics providers, transportation companies, and manufacturers.

Tourism and Hospitality: NEOM is expected to become a major tourism destination, attracting visitors with its futuristic attractions, sustainable living environments, and unique experiences.

Roshn: Addressing Housing Needs and Boosting Homeownership

Roshn, a large-scale residential housing project, is addressing Saudi Arabia's growing housing needs while aiming to increase homeownership rates. Roshn is developing integrated communities that offer a range of housing options, amenities, and services, catering to diverse income levels and lifestyles.

Opportunities for Businesses: Roshn creates opportunities for companies involved in:

Residential Construction: The construction of thousands of new homes requires expertise in residential construction, building materials, and interior design.

Real Estate Development and Management: Roshn's integrated communities require expertise in real estate development, property management, and community services.

Retail and Hospitality: Roshn's communities will feature retail spaces, restaurants, and entertainment venues, creating opportunities for businesses in these sectors.

Diriyah Gate: Preserving Heritage and Fostering Cultural Tourism

Diriyah Gate, a $20 billion project focused on restoring and revitalizing the historic city of Diriyah, is a testament to Saudi Arabia's commitment to preserving its cultural heritage. Diriyah, the birthplace of the first Saudi state, is being transformed into a world-class cultural and heritage destination.

Opportunities for Businesses: Diriyah Gate offers opportunities for companies specializing in:

Heritage Restoration and Conservation: The restoration of Diriyah's historic buildings and sites requires expertise in heritage conservation, architectural restoration, and traditional building techniques.

Cultural Tourism and Hospitality: Diriyah Gate is expected to become a major cultural tourism destination, attracting visitors with its museums, cultural centers, and traditional souks. This creates opportunities for hotels, restaurants, tour operators, and cultural event organizers.

Red Sea Global: Luxury Tourism with a Focus on Sustainability

Red Sea Global, a luxury tourism destination spanning 28,000 square kilometres along Saudi Arabia's Red Sea coast, is setting a new standard for sustainable tourism development. The project features a network of pristine islands, stunning beaches, and captivating inland destinations, offering a range of luxury accommodations, unforgettable experiences, and diverse activities.

Opportunities for Businesses: Red Sea Global presents a wealth of opportunities for companies in:

Luxury Hospitality and Resort Development: The construction and operation of luxury hotels, resorts, and villas require expertise in hospitality management, resort development, and the provision of high-end services. This includes opportunities for architects, interior designers, construction companies, and luxury brands seeking to establish a presence in this exclusive destination.

Sustainable Tourism and Environmental Management: Red Sea Global's unwavering commitment to sustainability creates opportunities for companies specializing in environmental management, renewable energy, and eco-friendly tourism practices. This includes expertise in waste management, water conservation, biodiversity protection, and the development of sustainable infrastructure.

Marine and Coastal Tourism: The Red Sea's rich marine life and pristine coral reefs make it a prime destination for diving, snorkeling, and other water sports. This creates opportunities for dive operators, boat tour companies, and marine conservation organizations.

Adventure and Experiential Tourism: Red Sea Global offers a range of adventure and experiential tourism activities, such as desert safaris, hiking, and cultural excursions. This creates opportunities for tour operators, adventure tourism companies, and cultural heritage organizations.

Qiddiya: A World-Class Entertainment, Sports, and Cultural Destination

Qiddiya, an $8 billion entertainment, sports, and cultural hub located just outside Riyadh, is poised to become a global destination for leisure and entertainment. The project features a theme park, water park, sports facilities, cultural venues, and a variety of dining and retail options.

Opportunities for Businesses: Qiddiya offers a multitude of opportunities for companies in:

Theme Park and Entertainment: The development and operation of Qiddiya's theme park and entertainment venues require expertise in theme park design, ride engineering, entertainment production, and hospitality management.

Sports and Recreation: Qiddiya's sports facilities, including a motorsports track, golf course, and equestrian center, create opportunities for sports equipment manufacturers, event organizers, and sports training academies.

Cultural and Performing Arts: Qiddiya's cultural venues, including a performing arts center and a museum, offer opportunities for cultural organizations, event promoters, and artists.

Hospitality and Retail: Qiddiya's hotels, restaurants, and retail outlets create opportunities for hospitality providers, restaurateurs, and retailers seeking to cater to a diverse and international clientele.

These giga-projects, along with others like the King Salman Park and the Amaala ultra-luxury resort, are transforming Saudi Arabia into a global hub for investment, innovation, and tourism. They offer a vast array of opportunities for international businesses seeking to participate in the Kingdom's ambitious economic transformation. By leveraging their expertise and partnering with local stakeholders, businesses can contribute to the success of these projects and capitalize on the immense growth potential of the Saudi market.

Navigating Saudi Arabia's Fiscal Landscape: A Balancing Act of Growth and Sustainability

Saudi Arabia faces fiscal challenges, a reality intertwined with its ambitious Vision 2030 plan. The Kingdom's return to a budget deficit in FY2023, driven by a confluence of lower oil revenue and increased spending, underscores the need for prudent fiscal management. However, the government is actively addressing these challenges, implementing a multi-pronged strategy aimed at balancing economic growth with long-term fiscal sustainability.

Fiscal Consolidation: A Gradual and Measured Approach

A consistent tightening of the fiscal stance over the medium term is vital to ensure a necessary measure of the long-term health of public finances. This consolidation is not about abrupt austerity, but rather a gradual and measured approach that prioritizes spending efficiency and targets areas where savings can be achieved without jeopardizing economic growth or social well-being.

Spending Rationalization: The government is focusing on rationalizing spending, particularly in areas such as:

Wage Bill: The wage bill, a significant portion of government spending, is being addressed through civil service reform, natural attrition, and a shift towards performance-based compensation. Further efforts to contain the wage bill, including benchmarking public sector wages to private sector levels to reduce the wage premium is essential.

Subsidies: Fuel subsidies, while providing social benefits, represent a significant fiscal burden. The government has taken steps to reduce these subsidies, further reforms are encouraged, including lifting the cap on gasoline prices and implementing targeted social programs to mitigate the impact on vulnerable households.

Public Investment Management: Strengthening public investment management is crucial to ensure that government investments generate high returns and contribute to economic growth. Enhancing project appraisal and selection processes, improving cost controls, and promoting transparency and accountability in public investment projects are also recommended.

The IMF stresses the importance of sequencing fiscal consolidation measures carefully to avoid undermining economic growth. The report recommends prioritizing non-oil revenue mobilization and spending rationalization over sharp cuts in capital spending, which could have adverse effects on long-term growth prospects.

Revenue Mobilization: Broadening the Tax Base and Enhancing Efficiency

Increasing non-oil revenue is essential to reduce the Kingdom's reliance on oil income and create a more stable and sustainable fiscal base. The government is exploring various options to enhance revenue mobilization, including:

Introduction of New Taxes: Introducing a property tax and a personal income tax, which are common revenue sources in many countries are vital. These taxes could generate significant revenue while broadening the tax base and reducing reliance on oil income.

Reform of Existing Taxes: The government is also considering reforms to existing taxes, such as expat levies, excises, and corporate taxes, to enhance their efficiency and revenue-generating potential. This includes addressing VAT policy gaps and reviewing tax incentives to ensure they are effective and aligned with broader economic objectives.

Strengthening Tax Administration: Improving tax administration is crucial to ensure that taxes are collected efficiently and fairly. strengthening tax compliance, streamlining tax procedures, and leveraging technology to enhance tax collection processes are all recommended.

Strengthening Fiscal Institutions: Enhancing Transparency, Accountability, and Long-Term Planning

Strengthening fiscal institutions is vital to ensure sound fiscal management and promote long-term fiscal sustainability. The government is taking steps to enhance fiscal institutions, including:

Developing a Medium-Term Fiscal Framework (MTFF): The MTFF will provide a multi-year perspective on fiscal policy, outlining revenue and spending plans, deficit targets, and a fiscal anchor to guide policy decisions. This will enhance transparency, accountability, and long-term fiscal planning.

Enhancing Fiscal Risk Management: The government is developing a comprehensive fiscal risk framework to identify, assess, and manage fiscal risks, including those arising from oil price volatility, contingent liabilities, and public-private partnerships. This will strengthen the government's ability to mitigate fiscal risks and ensure the sustainability of public finances.

Operationalizing a Fiscal Rule: The government is working to operationalize a fiscal rule to delink spending from oil price fluctuations. This will help to smooth government spending over time, reduce procyclicality, and enhance fiscal sustainability. It is recommended to introduce an expenditure rule that integrates a ceiling on expenditure growth and a target for the Central Government Net Financial Assets (CGNFA).

Saudi Arabia's fiscal landscape is undergoing a significant transformation as the government navigates the complexities of balancing ambitious growth objectives with the imperative of long-term fiscal sustainability. While acknowledging the challenges, it is of high importance for the government to actively engage in addressing these challenges through a combination of fiscal consolidation, revenue mobilization, and institutional strengthening.

These measures are not merely about balancing the books; they are about building a more resilient and diversified economy that can weather the inevitable fluctuations in oil prices and global economic conditions. By demonstrating a commitment to fiscal responsibility and transparency, the government aims to foster investor confidence, attract foreign capital, and ensure that the benefits of economic growth are shared equitably across generations.

The path ahead will require continued commitment to reform, careful calibration of policies, and a willingness to adapt to changing circumstances. However, Saudi Arabia is on the right track, laying the groundwork for a fiscally sound and sustainable future.

A Favourable Investment Climate: Saudi Arabia Opens its Doors to the World

Saudi Arabia is actively courting foreign investors, recognizing their vital role in driving economic diversification and achieving the ambitious goals of Vision 2030. This welcoming stance is reflected in the Kingdom's improved ranking in the IMD's World Competitiveness Index, a testament to the government's ongoing efforts to create a more business-friendly environment.

Business-Friendly Reforms: Streamlining the Path to Investment

The government has implemented a series of business-friendly reforms aimed at reducing barriers to entry, streamlining regulations, and enhancing the ease of doing business. These reforms include:

Streamlined Regulations: The government has simplified and streamlined regulations across various sectors, reducing bureaucracy and making it easier for businesses to obtain licenses and permits. The introduction of the new law on civil transactions, for example, provides greater certainty and predictability in contract enforcement, financial transactions, and property rights.

Reduced Bureaucracy: The government has digitized many government services, making it easier for businesses to interact with government agencies and reducing the time and cost of doing business. The Etimad platform, for example, has significantly reduced payment delays for private sector contractors.

Improved Access to Land and Financing: The government is working to improve access to land for industrial and commercial development, as well as expanding access to finance for businesses, particularly small and medium-sized enterprises (SMEs).

Regional Headquarters Program: Attracting Global Players

The Regional Headquarters Program is a strategic initiative designed to attract multinational companies to establish their regional headquarters in Saudi Arabia. The program offers a range of incentives, including:

Tax Benefits: Companies establishing regional headquarters in Saudi Arabia can benefit from tax incentives, such as reduced corporate income tax rates and exemptions from certain taxes.

Regulatory Flexibility: Regional headquarters can benefit from greater regulatory flexibility, including exemptions from certain Saudization requirements.

Access to Talent: Saudi Arabia's growing pool of skilled talent, particularly in sectors such as technology and finance, is a major draw for multinational companies.

Special Economic Zones (SEZs): Creating Hubs for Investment and Innovation

Special Economic Zones (SEZs) are designated areas that offer a range of incentives to attract foreign investment and promote economic activity. Saudi Arabia is developing several SEZs, each with its own unique focus and advantages. These SEZs offer:

Tax Benefits: Businesses operating in SEZs can benefit from tax incentives, such as reduced corporate income tax rates, exemptions from import duties, and tax holidays.

Regulatory Flexibility: SEZs offer greater regulatory flexibility, including exemptions from certain labor laws and Saudization requirements.

Infrastructure and Logistics: SEZs are typically equipped with world-class infrastructure and logistics facilities, making it easier for businesses to operate and connect with global markets.

Opportunities Amidst Transformation: Capitalizing on a Dynamic Market

Saudi Arabia's economic transformation is creating a wealth of opportunities for foreign investors across a range of sectors. Key opportunities include:

Digitalization: Saudi Arabia is a leader in digital transformation, with a rapidly growing digital economy and a thriving fintech ecosystem. This creates opportunities for companies specializing in digital services, e-commerce, fintech, and artificial intelligence.

Renewable Energy: The Kingdom is committed to achieving net-zero emissions by 2060, with ambitious plans for renewable energy, energy efficiency, and green finance. This creates opportunities for companies involved in solar and wind energy, energy storage, and green technology.

Financial Services: Saudi Arabia's robust and well-capitalized banking sector, coupled with a growing fintech ecosystem, offers opportunities for financial institutions and investors. This includes opportunities in retail banking, investment banking, asset management, and insurance.

Tourism: With the tourism sector projected to contribute 16% to GDP by 2034, opportunities abound for tourism operators, hospitality providers, and related businesses. This includes opportunities in luxury hospitality, sustainable tourism, cultural tourism, and adventure tourism.

Saudi Arabia's efforts to create a more favourable investment climate are paying off, as evidenced by the growing influx of foreign investment and the increasing number of multinational companies establishing a presence in the Kingdom. By continuing to implement business-friendly reforms, promoting strategic initiatives like the Regional Headquarters Program and SEZs, and capitalizing on the opportunities created by its economic transformation, Saudi Arabia is positioning itself as a leading destination for foreign investment and a key player in the global economy.

Saudi Arabia's Investment Landscape: Targeted Opportunities for Growth

Within the Saudi Arabia's economic transformation landscape, specific areas ripe for investment can be identified. These areas align with the Kingdom's strategic priorities under Vision 2030, offering investors the chance to participate in a dynamic and evolving market with significant growth potential.

Digitalization: A Technological Leap Forward

Saudi Arabia is rapidly embracing digital technologies, positioning itself as a regional leader in digital transformation. The Kingdom's impressive progress in digitalization, creating a wealth of opportunities for investors in:

Fintech: Saudi Arabia's burgeoning fintech ecosystem is attracting significant investment, with opportunities for companies specializing in payments, lending, insurance, and wealth management. It is noteworthy to mention the positive impact of SAMA's regulatory sandboxes and partnerships with international fintech companies in fostering innovation in this sector.

Digital Service Providers: The demand for digital services is soaring in Saudi Arabia, creating opportunities for companies providing cloud computing, cybersecurity, data analytics, and e-commerce solutions. The government's push for e-government services and the increasing adoption of digital technologies by businesses are driving this growth.

Artificial Intelligence (AI): Saudi Arabia is making significant investments in AI technologies, aiming to leverage AI to enhance productivity, drive economic diversification, and improve public services. It is also noted that Saudi Arabia is favorably positioned in AI readiness, comparable to high-income countries. This creates opportunities for companies developing AI solutions for various sectors, including healthcare, education, transportation, and energy.

Renewable Energy: A Sustainable Path to Energy Security

The Kingdom is committed to achieving net-zero emissions by 2060, a goal that is driving significant investments in renewable energy, energy efficiency, and green finance. These initiatives are of high importance, highlighting opportunities for investors in:

Renewable Energy Projects: Saudi Arabia's ambitious plans for solar and wind energy projects create opportunities for developers, investors, and technology providers. The government's target of generating 50% of its electricity from renewable sources by 2030 is driving a rapid expansion of renewable energy capacity.

Energy Efficiency Solutions: Improving energy efficiency is a key component of Saudi Arabia's sustainability strategy. This creates opportunities for companies providing energy efficiency solutions for buildings, industries, and transportation. The Saudi Energy Efficiency Program (SEEP) is driving the adoption of energy-efficient technologies and practices across various sectors.

Green Finance: The growth of green finance is supporting Saudi Arabia's transition to a more sustainable economy. This creates opportunities for investors in green bonds, sustainable investment funds, and other financial instruments that support renewable energy and other green projects. The positive impact of Saudi Arabia's inaugural sovereign green bond issuance in mobilizing private capital for green investments is also noticeable.

Financial Services: A Robust and Evolving Sector

Saudi Arabia's financial services sector is characterized by a robust and well-capitalized banking sector, a growing fintech ecosystem, and a supportive regulatory environment. The resilience of the banking sector is also noticeable, its strong solvency and liquidity ratios point to opportunities for investors in:

Traditional Banking: Saudi Arabia's banking sector offers opportunities for traditional banking services, including retail banking, corporate banking, and investment banking. Further efforts to strengthen the supervisory framework and enhance financial safety nets are encouraged.

Fintech: The growth of fintech is creating new opportunities in areas such as payments, lending, and wealth management. It is also recommended to continue the support for the development of the fintech ecosystem, including through regulatory sandboxes and partnerships with international fintech companies.

Islamic Finance: Saudi Arabia is a global leader in Islamic finance, offering opportunities for investors in Islamic banking, sukuk (Islamic bonds), and other Islamic financial instruments. Ensuring effective implementation of regulations related to Islamic banking and managing liquidity risk separately for Islamic windows is also of critical importance.

Tourism: A Sector Poised for Exponential Growth

Saudi Arabia's tourism sector is experiencing a remarkable transformation, fuelled by the government's ambition to make the Kingdom a global tourism powerhouse. The IMF projects the sector to contribute a substantial 16% to GDP by 2034, highlighting its immense growth potential. This potential is underpinned by several factors:

Easing of Visa Restrictions: The introduction of tourist e-visas has significantly simplified the process for international travellers to visit Saudi Arabia, opening the doors to a wider range of tourists.

Development of New Destinations: Mega-projects like the Red Sea Global, Qiddiya, and Amaala are creating world-class tourism destinations, offering a diverse range of experiences, from luxury resorts and adventure activities to cultural attractions and historical sites.

Promotion of Cultural Heritage: Saudi Arabia is actively showcasing its rich cultural heritage, promoting its ancient cities, historical sites, and unique traditions. This attracts cultural tourists seeking authentic experiences and diversifies the tourism sector beyond religious tourism.

These developments create a wealth of opportunities for investors in:

Luxury Hospitality: The construction and operation of luxury hotels, resorts, and villas require expertise in hospitality management, resort development, and the provision of high-end services. This includes opportunities for architects, interior designers, construction companies, and luxury brands seeking to establish a presence in this burgeoning market.

Sustainable Tourism: Saudi Arabia is committed to developing its tourism sector sustainably, creating opportunities for companies specializing in eco-friendly tourism practices, environmental management, and renewable energy solutions.

Experiential Tourism: The Kingdom's diverse landscapes and cultural heritage offer a rich tapestry of experiences, from desert safaris and adventure activities to cultural tours and historical explorations. This creates opportunities for tour operators, adventure tourism companies, and cultural heritage organizations.

Tourism Infrastructure: The growth of the tourism sector requires significant investment in infrastructure, including airports, transportation networks, and hospitality facilities. This creates opportunities for construction companies, engineering firms, and logistics providers.

The Kingdom's commitment to economic transformation, coupled with its targeted investments in key sectors like digitalization, renewable energy, financial services, and tourism, creates a unique and attractive investment landscape.

By aligning their investments with Saudi Arabia's strategic priorities, investors can not only capitalize on the Kingdom's growth potential but also contribute to its ambitious vision of a diversified, sustainable, and globally competitive economy.

Key Takeaways for Investors: A Roadmap to Success in Saudi Arabia

While the Kingdom offers a wealth of opportunities, it's crucial for investors to approach the market strategically, with a clear understanding of the risks and rewards. Here are key takeaways from the report to guide investors towards success:

Due Diligence: Navigating Risks and Opportunities

Thorough due diligence is paramount for any investment decision, and this is particularly true in a rapidly transforming market like

Saudi Arabia. Investors must carefully assess both the opportunities and the risks, taking into account the following factors:

Fiscal Risks: Investors should carefully assess the potential impact of fiscal challenges on specific projects, considering factors such as government spending priorities, revenue mobilization plans, and the sustainability of public finances.

Global Economic Shifts: The global economic landscape is constantly evolving, and investors must consider the potential impact of global economic shifts on their investments in Saudi Arabia. This includes factors such as oil price volatility, global trade tensions, and changes in monetary policy by major central banks.

Sector-Specific Risks: Each sector has its own unique set of risks and opportunities. Investors should conduct thorough research on the specific sectors they are considering, understanding the regulatory environment, competitive landscape, and growth potential of each sector.

Partnerships: Leveraging Local Expertise and Networks

Collaboration with local partners is essential for navigating the Saudi Arabian market. Local partners can provide valuable insights into the regulatory environment, cultural nuances, and business practices, as well as access to local networks and resources.

Navigating the Regulatory Environment: Saudi Arabia's regulatory environment is complex and evolving. Local partners can help investors understand the relevant regulations, obtain necessary licenses and permits, and ensure compliance with local laws.

Understanding Cultural Nuances: Saudi Arabia has a unique culture and business etiquette. Local partners can help investors navigate cultural sensitivities, build relationships with key stakeholders, and avoid potential misunderstandings.

Accessing Local Networks and Resources: Local partners can provide access to local networks, suppliers, distributors, and other resources that can be invaluable for businesses operating in Saudi Arabia.

Long-Term Vision: Aligning with Vision 2030

Investors should focus on projects that are aligned with the Kingdom's long-term vision for economic transformation, as outlined in Vision 2030. This means prioritizing projects that:

Support Economic Diversification: Vision 2030 aims to reduce Saudi Arabia's reliance on oil and develop a more diversified economy. Investors should seek opportunities in sectors that are aligned with this goal, such as technology, tourism, renewable energy, and manufacturing.

Promote Private Sector Growth: The government is actively encouraging private sector participation in the economy. Investors should focus on projects that contribute to private sector growth, creating jobs, fostering innovation, and enhancing competitiveness.

Enhance Sustainability: Sustainability is a core principle of Vision 2030. Investors should prioritize projects that promote environmental sustainability, social responsibility, and good governance.

Investing in Saudi Arabia requires a strategic approach, combining thorough due diligence, strong local partnerships, and a long-term vision aligned with the Kingdom's transformative goals. By following these key takeaways, investors can position themselves for success in a dynamic and evolving market with immense potential.

Chapter conclusion: A Call to Action for Investors in Saudi Arabia

Saudi Arabia's economic transformation, guided by the ambitious Vision 2030 plan, presents a compelling and unique opportunity for investors seeking growth and diversification. The Kingdom is embarking on a journey of unprecedented change, reshaping its economy, society, and its place in the world. This transformation is not without its challenges, but the IMF report provides valuable insights for navigating this dynamic market and capitalizing on its immense potential.

For investors, the key takeaway is clear: Saudi Arabia is a land of opportunity, but success requires a strategic approach. Careful planning, thorough due diligence, and a long-term vision aligned with Vision 2030 are essential. The IMF report provides a roadmap for investors, highlighting specific sectors ripe for investment, emphasizing the importance of strong local partnerships, and underscoring the need to navigate risks and opportunities with prudence.

A Transformative Journey: More Than Just Returns

Investing in Saudi Arabia is not merely about seeking financial returns; it is about participating in a transformative journey that is reshaping the Kingdom and the region. Investors can contribute to Saudi Arabia's sustainable development, supporting its economic diversification, fostering private sector growth, and promoting social progress.

By aligning their investments with Vision 2030, investors can play a vital role in building a more prosperous and sustainable future for Saudi Arabia. The Kingdom's commitment to innovation, technology, and sustainability creates a fertile ground for investments that can generate both financial returns and positive social impact.

The Kingdom's leadership is committed to creating a welcoming environment for foreign investment, and the opportunities are vast and diverse.

With careful planning, strategic partnerships, and a long-term vision, investors can capitalize on Saudi Arabia's potential and contribute to its sustainable development, forging a path towards shared prosperity and a brighter future for the Kingdom and its people.

Bahaa G. Arnouk

Qatar: A Rising Star in the Gulf

Qatar dazzled the world with its hosting of the 2022 FIFA World Cup, but the nation's ambitions reach far beyond the football pitch. Qatar is on a compelling journey of economic transformation. This chapter highlights Qatar's robust growth, strategic diversification efforts, and a stable investment climate that is attracting global attention. It also explores the exciting opportunities emerging in Qatar's dynamic economy and the key sectors poised for growth.

Beyond Gas: A Diversification Strategy in Action

While the hydrocarbon sector remains a cornerstone of the Qatari economy, the nation is actively pursuing a multifaceted diversification strategy. This commitment to broadening the economic base is evident in several key areas:

Robust Non-Hydrocarbon Growth:

The IMF report underscores the significant contribution of non-hydrocarbon sectors to Qatar's economic expansion. This growth is not merely incidental but a result of deliberate policy decisions and substantial investments.

Public Project Investments: Qatar has channeled significant resources into public projects, particularly infrastructure development. This includes investments in transportation networks, such as the Doha Metro and Hamad International Airport, as well as projects related to healthcare, education, and social services. These investments have not only enhanced the quality of life for residents but have also created a more attractive environment for businesses and investors.

North Field LNG Expansion Project: While technically within the hydrocarbon sector, the construction phase of the North Field LNG expansion project has generated substantial economic activity in non-hydrocarbon sectors. This includes demand for construction materials, logistics services, and a range of support industries, creating a positive spillover effect throughout the economy.

Thriving Tourism Sector:

Qatar's tourism sector is experiencing a remarkable transformation, capitalising on the legacy of the 2022 World Cup. The nation's successful hosting of the tournament has significantly enhanced its global visibility, attracting a new wave of tourists eager to experience Qatar's unique offerings.

World Cup Legacy: The infrastructure developed for the World Cup, including state-of-the-art stadiums, hotels, and transportation networks, has created a solid foundation for the tourism sector.

Proactive Tourism Initiatives: Qatar is actively pursuing initiatives to attract visitors, such as visa facilitation, promotional campaigns targeting key markets, and the development of new tourist attractions.

Post-World Cup Resilience: The resilience of the tourism sector post-World Cup, with visitor numbers in 2023 exceeding pre-pandemic levels is acknowledged. This indicates the sustainability of the tourism boom and its potential to contribute significantly to economic diversification.

Third National Development Strategy (NDS3):

The upcoming NDS3 is poised to be a game-changer for Qatar's economic diversification efforts. This comprehensive strategy will provide a detailed roadmap for the nation's economic transformation over the coming years.

Private Sector-Led Growth: NDS3 will prioritize fostering a more vibrant and dynamic private sector, recognizing its crucial role in driving sustainable economic growth and diversification.

Innovation and Technology: The strategy will emphasize promoting innovation and technological advancement, positioning Qatar as a regional hub for knowledge-based industries.

Human Capital Development: NDS3 will focus on enhancing human capital development, ensuring that Qatar's workforce is equipped with the skills and knowledge necessary to thrive in a diversified economy.

Growth Projections:

The IMF projects medium-term growth to average around 5.5%, fuelled by the North Field expansion and the implementation of NDS3. This robust growth outlook is a testament to the effectiveness of Qatar's diversification strategy and its ability to attract foreign investment. The positive assessment reinforces the view that Qatar is on the right track to achieve its diversification goals.

In conclusion, Qatar's commitment to economic diversification goes beyond mere rhetoric. The nation is taking concrete steps to reduce its reliance on hydrocarbons and foster a more balanced and sustainable economy.

North Field Expansion: A Cornerstone of Growth

The North Field LNG expansion project, a massive undertaking of unprecedented scale, is poised to be a cornerstone of Qatar's future economic growth. Set to significantly increase Qatar's LNG production capacity by 2028, this project represents a multi-billion-dollar opportunity for international businesses across a wide spectrum of sectors.

A Mega-Project with Global Implications:

Scale and Scope: The North Field expansion is not merely an incremental increase in production but a transformative project that will solidify Qatar's position as a global LNG powerhouse. The project involves the development of new offshore platforms, onshore processing facilities, and export infrastructure, requiring a massive influx of investment and expertise.

Economic Catalyst: The sheer scale of the project has a ripple effect throughout the Qatari economy, stimulating growth in numerous sectors. The demand for construction materials, specialized equipment, logistics services, and a range of support industries is creating a surge in economic activity.

Opportunities for International Businesses:

Construction and Engineering: The construction phase of the North Field expansion presents a golden opportunity for international construction and engineering firms. The project requires expertise in a range of specialized areas, including offshore platform construction, pipeline installation, and the development of complex processing facilities.

Technology and Innovation: The expansion project is leveraging cutting-edge technologies to enhance efficiency, productivity, and environmental performance. This creates opportunities for technology providers, equipment manufacturers, and innovators to contribute their expertise and solutions to this groundbreaking project.

Financial Services: The financing of the North Field expansion requires sophisticated financial services, including project finance, insurance, and risk management. International financial institutions and investors have a significant role to play in supporting the project's financial needs.

Meeting Global LNG Demand:

Increasing Global Demand: The expansion comes at a time of increasing global demand for LNG, particularly from Asia and Europe. The shift towards cleaner energy sources, coupled with geopolitical factors, has driven a surge in demand for LNG, positioning Qatar to capitalize on this trend.

Securing Long-Term Contracts: Qatar has been proactive in securing long-term LNG supply contracts with key customers in Asia and Europe, ensuring a stable and predictable revenue stream from the North Field expansion. These contracts provide a solid foundation for Qatar's long-term economic growth.

Strategic Importance: The expansion will not only boost Qatar's economic growth but also enhance its strategic importance as a reliable and stable supplier of LNG to global markets. This reinforces Qatar's position as a key player in the global energy landscape.

Solidifying Qatar's LNG Leadership:

Production Capacity: The North Field expansion will significantly increase Qatar's LNG production capacity, further cementing its position as a leading LNG exporter. This increased capacity will enable Qatar to meet the growing global demand for LNG and maintain its competitive edge in the market.

Technological Advancement: The project is driving technological advancements in the LNG sector, enhancing Qatar's reputation as a leader in innovation and efficiency. This will further strengthen Qatar's position as a preferred LNG supplier for global customers.

Economic Diversification: While the North Field expansion is primarily within the hydrocarbon sector, its impact on the broader economy is contributing to Qatar's diversification efforts. The project's spillover effects are stimulating growth in non-hydrocarbon sectors, supporting the development of a more balanced and resilient economy.

In conclusion, the North Field LNG expansion project is a transformative undertaking that will have a profound impact on Qatar's economic future. The project presents a multitude of opportunities for international businesses, while also contributing to Qatar's economic diversification and solidifying its position as a global LNG leader.

Navigating the Fiscal Landscape

Qatar delivered an impressive track record of fiscal prudence, demonstrated by the consistent achievement of significant fiscal and current account surpluses in recent years. This fiscal strength is a testament to the nation's sound economic management and its commitment to responsible spending. However, maintaining this fiscal discipline is crucial, especially as Qatar embarks on an ambitious economic transformation agenda. The IMF outlines a clear path for navigating this fiscal landscape, balancing prudence with the need to support diversification and long-term growth.

Sustained Fiscal Prudence:

Permanent Income Hypothesis (PIH) as a Guiding Principle: Adhering to a fiscal anchor based on the Permanent Income Hypothesis (PIH) is critical. This principle advocates for a sustainable spending path that aligns with long-term revenue expectations, rather than being swayed by short-term fluctuations in hydrocarbon revenues.

Intergenerational Equity: The PIH framework ensures intergenerational equity, meaning that current hydrocarbon wealth is managed responsibly to benefit future generations. This prevents excessive spending that could deplete resources and jeopardize the economic well-being of future Qataris.

Resilience Against External Shocks: A PIH-based fiscal anchor enhances Qatar's resilience against external shocks, particularly volatility in global energy prices. By smoothing spending over time, Qatar can avoid sharp adjustments in response to price fluctuations, ensuring greater economic stability.

Operationalizing Fiscal Prudence: The report suggests several practical measures to operationalize fiscal prudence:

Conservative Revenue Projections: Basing budget projections on conservative oil and gas price assumptions, avoiding overestimation of future revenues.

Contingency Planning: Establishing robust contingency plans to address potential revenue shortfalls due to unforeseen circumstances.

Fiscal Buffers: Maintaining adequate fiscal reserves to provide a cushion against unexpected shocks and ensure fiscal sustainability.

Revenue Diversification:

Broadening the Revenue Base: The importance of diversifying Qatar's revenue sources, reducing reliance on hydrocarbon revenues, which are inherently volatile and subject to long-term decline as the world transitions to cleaner energy sources is paramount.

Introducing a Value Added Tax (VAT): The report recommends the introduction of a broad-based VAT as a key measure to modernize the tax system and broaden the revenue base. A VAT would provide a stable and predictable source of non-hydrocarbon revenue, enhancing fiscal sustainability.

Implementation Readiness: Qatar has made significant progress in preparing for VAT implementation, including developing the necessary administrative infrastructure and legal framework.

Social Impact Mitigation: The report suggests that the introduction of VAT be accompanied by measures to mitigate any potential adverse impact on low-income households, such as targeted social safety net programs.

Exploring Other Revenue Sources: In addition to VAT, Qatar is encouraged to explore other potential sources of non-hydrocarbon revenue, such as property taxes, excise taxes, and environmental levies.

Expenditure Optimization:

A strategic approach to expenditure optimization is required, focusing on enhancing efficiency, promoting sustainability, and aligning spending with Qatar's long-term economic transformation goals. This involves a multi-pronged approach:

Enhancing Spending Efficiency: The report recommends a comprehensive review of government spending to identify areas for efficiency improvements and cost savings. This involves:

Performance-Based Budgeting: Shifting towards a performance-based budgeting approach, linking budget allocations to specific outcomes and performance targets. This ensures that funding is directed towards programs and initiatives that deliver tangible results and contribute to national priorities.

Public Procurement Reform: Strengthening public procurement processes to ensure transparency, competition, and value for money. This involves streamlining procurement procedures, promoting open and competitive bidding, and implementing robust monitoring mechanisms to prevent corruption and ensure efficient use of public funds.

Rationalizing the Public Wage Bill: Recognizing the significant share of the public wage bill in government spending, the report recommends measures to ensure its sustainability and efficiency:

Wage Structure Review: Conducting a comprehensive review of the public sector wage structure to ensure alignment with market rates and promote efficiency. This involves benchmarking public sector salaries against comparable positions in the private sector, addressing any disparities, and ensuring that compensation is competitive while remaining fiscally sustainable.

Employment Growth Management: Implementing measures to manage the growth of public sector employment, focusing on essential services and aligning hiring with strategic priorities. This involves prioritizing recruitment in key sectors, such as education, healthcare, and technology, while exercising restraint in non-essential areas.

Phasing Out Subsidies: The gradual phasing out of remaining subsidies is encouraged, particularly on energy. This would not only reduce government spending but also promote more efficient resource allocation and encourage the adoption of cleaner energy sources.

Targeted Approach: A targeted approach to subsidy removal is essential, focusing on those subsidies that are most distortive and least beneficial to vulnerable households.

Social Safety Nets: The removal of subsidies should be accompanied by strengthened social safety net programs to protect low-income households from any potential adverse impact on their living standards.

Communication and Transparency: Effective communication and transparency are crucial to build public understanding and support for subsidy reform. This involves clearly explaining the rationale for subsidy removal, the benefits of reform, and the measures taken to mitigate any negative social impact.

Reorienting Spending Towards Growth-Enhancing Reforms: Reorienting government spending towards reforms that promote private sector-led growth and economic diversification is also recommended. This involves strategic investments in:

- **Human Capital Development**: Education, training, and skills development are crucial for building a highly skilled and adaptable workforce, capable of driving innovation and productivity in a diversified economy.

- **Research and Development**: Investing in research and development fosters innovation, technological advancement, and the development of new industries, enhancing Qatar's competitiveness in the global economy.

- **Infrastructure**: Targeted infrastructure investments, particularly in transportation, logistics, and digital connectivity, can enhance productivity, reduce business costs, and attract foreign investment.

- **Business Environment Reforms**: Streamlining regulations, improving the ease of doing business, and promoting competition create a more conducive environment for private sector growth and investment.

By adopting a strategic approach to expenditure optimization, Qatar can ensure that its fiscal resources are used effectively to support economic transformation, enhance long-term sustainability, and secure a prosperous future for its citizens.

A Stable and Secure Investment Climate

Qatar presents a compelling proposition for foreign investors seeking a stable and secure environment to deploy their capital. The nation's appeal stems from a confluence of factors, including robust macroeconomic fundamentals, prudent policymaking, and a proactive approach to structural reforms. The progress made in enhancing labor market flexibility is noticeable, improving the business environment, and promoting digital transformation, further solidifying Qatar's attractiveness as an investment destination.

Strong & Resilient Macroeconomic Fundamentals:

Fiscal Strength: Qatar's consistent fiscal surpluses, underpinned by prudent spending and a commitment to long-term sustainability, provide a solid foundation for economic stability. This fiscal strength reduces the risk of sovereign debt distress and creates a more predictable and secure environment for investors.

External Stability: Qatar's substantial current account surpluses, driven by robust hydrocarbon exports and a growing non-hydrocarbon sector, contribute to a strong external position. This reduces vulnerability to external shocks and reinforces investor confidence.

Stable Currency: The Qatari Riyal's peg to the US dollar provides currency stability, reducing exchange rate risk for foreign investors. This predictability enhances the attractiveness of Qatar as an investment destination, particularly for long-term projects.

Low Inflation: Qatar has a track record of maintaining low and stable inflation, creating a more predictable environment for businesses and investors. This price stability enhances business planning and reduces uncertainty.

Attractive Business Environment:

Streamlined Regulations: Qatar has made significant strides in streamlining regulations and reducing bureaucratic hurdles for businesses. This includes simplifying business registration processes, reducing the number of permits and licenses required, and enhancing transparency in regulatory frameworks.

Enhanced Administrative Efficiency: The government is committed to improving administrative efficiency, reducing processing times for applications and approvals, and enhancing the overall ease of doing business. This includes leveraging digital technologies to streamline processes and improve service delivery.

Public-Private Partnerships (PPPs): Qatar actively promotes public-private partnerships (PPPs) as a mechanism to leverage private sector expertise and capital for infrastructure development and other strategic projects. The PPP framework provides a clear and transparent structure for collaboration between the government and private investors.

Investor Protection: Qatar has a robust legal framework that protects the rights of foreign investors, ensuring a level playing field and fair treatment. The nation's commitment to upholding the rule of law enhances investor confidence and security.

Strong Financial Sector:

Well-Capitalized Banks: Qatar's banking sector is characterized by well-capitalized and liquid banks, providing a solid foundation for financial stability and investor confidence. The banks have strong balance sheets, robust risk management practices, and are well-regulated by the Qatar Central Bank.

Deepening Capital Markets: Qatar is actively developing its domestic capital markets, providing alternative sources of financing for businesses and investors. This includes initiatives to promote the issuance of bonds and sukuk, as well as the development of a more vibrant stock market.

Fintech Innovation: Qatar is embracing fintech innovation, creating a more dynamic and competitive financial services landscape. The launch of a National Fintech Strategy aims to foster innovation, attract fintech companies, and enhance financial inclusion.

Strategic Location and World-Class Infrastructure:

Geographic Advantage: Qatar's strategic location at the crossroads of major trade routes between Asia, Europe, and Africa makes it a natural hub for regional and international trade. This geographic advantage is further enhanced by:

World-Class Infrastructure: Qatar boasts world-class infrastructure, including a modern transportation network, a state-of-the-art airport, and a well-developed logistics sector. This infrastructure facilitates the movement of goods and people, reducing business costs and enhancing connectivity.

Free Trade Zones: Qatar has established several free trade zones that offer tax incentives, streamlined regulations, and other benefits to attract foreign investment and promote international trade.

In conclusion, Qatar's commitment to creating a stable and secure investment climate is evident in its strong macroeconomic fundamentals, its proactive approach to structural reforms, and its ongoing efforts to enhance the business environment.

Opportunities in a Transforming Economy

Qatar's ambitious economic transformation agenda, coupled with its commitment to sustainability and innovation, presents a wealth of opportunities for foreign investors seeking to capitalize on the nation's dynamic growth trajectory. Several key sectors ripe for investment can be highlighted, offering promising prospects for those seeking to contribute to Qatar's long-term prosperity.

Digitalization:

Rapid Digital Transformation: Qatar has made remarkable progress in digital transformation, establishing itself as a regional leader in digital infrastructure and services. This progress is driven by a strategic vision to leverage technology for economic growth, social development, and government efficiency.

National Fintech Strategy: The launch of a National Fintech Strategy underscores Qatar's commitment to fostering innovation in the financial services sector. The strategy aims to create a thriving fintech ecosystem, attracting fintech companies, promoting collaboration, and enhancing financial inclusion.

Investment Opportunities: This presents significant investment opportunities for fintech companies, digital service providers, technology innovators, and venture capitalists seeking to capitalize on Qatar's burgeoning fintech landscape.

E-Government Initiatives: Qatar has implemented comprehensive e-government initiatives, streamlining government services, enhancing transparency, and improving citizen engagement. This digitalization drive creates opportunities for companies specializing in e-government solutions, cybersecurity, and data analytics.

Smart City Development: Qatar is investing in smart city development, leveraging technology to enhance urban living, improve sustainability, and optimize resource management. This presents opportunities for companies involved in smart city technologies, such as IoT, AI, and big data analytics.

Renewable Energy:

Commitment to Climate Action: Qatar is committed to addressing climate change and transitioning to a more sustainable energy future. This commitment is guided by the National Environment and Climate Change Strategy, which outlines ambitious targets for reducing greenhouse gas emissions and promoting renewable energy.

Solar Energy Potential: Qatar has abundant solar energy potential, making it an ideal location for developing solar power projects. The government is actively encouraging investments in solar energy, providing incentives, and creating a favourable regulatory environment.

Energy Efficiency: Qatar is also focusing on enhancing energy efficiency across various sectors, including buildings, transportation, and industry. This presents opportunities for companies specializing in energy efficiency technologies, building retrofits, and sustainable transportation solutions.

Green Finance: The development of green finance mechanisms is crucial for supporting Qatar's transition to a low-carbon economy. This presents opportunities for financial institutions, investors, and green bond issuers to contribute to Qatar's sustainability agenda.

Tourism and Hospitality:

World Cup Legacy: The 2022 World Cup has left a lasting legacy on Qatar's tourism sector, significantly enhancing its global visibility and attracting a new wave of visitors. The infrastructure developed for the tournament, including state-of-the-art stadiums, hotels, and transportation networks, provides a solid foundation for future growth.

Tourism Diversification: Qatar is actively diversifying its tourism offerings, moving beyond traditional attractions to develop niche tourism segments, such as cultural tourism, sports tourism, and eco-tourism. This creates opportunities for tourism operators, hospitality providers, and related businesses to cater to a wider range of visitor interests.

Hospitality Infrastructure: The ongoing expansion of hospitality infrastructure, including new hotels, resorts, and entertainment facilities, presents investment opportunities for hotel chains, property developers, and hospitality management companies.

Regional Tourism Hub: Qatar's strategic location and world-class airport make it a convenient hub for regional tourism, providing opportunities for tour operators and travel agencies to develop multi-destination itineraries that include Qatar.

Human Capital Development:

Skills for a Diversified Economy: As Qatar transitions to a more diversified and knowledge-based economy, investments in human capital development are crucial for ensuring that the workforce is equipped with the skills and knowledge necessary to thrive in the new economic landscape.

Education and Training: Investment opportunities exist in education and training institutions, particularly those offering specialized programs in areas such as technology, engineering, finance, and tourism.

Skills Development Programs: Companies specializing in skills development and vocational training can play a vital role in upskilling and reskilling the workforce to meet the evolving demands of the labor market.

Lifelong Learning: Promoting a culture of lifelong learning is essential for ensuring that Qatar's workforce remains adaptable and competitive in the face of rapid technological advancements and changing industry needs.

Key Takeaways for Investors

Qatar's economic transformation presents a compelling opportunity for foreign investors, but success requires a strategic approach, a commitment to partnership, and a long-term perspective. Key takeaways for investors seeking to capitalize on Qatar's promising future.

Strategic Alignment:

NDS3 and QNV 2030 as Guiding Frameworks: Investors should prioritize projects and initiatives that align with Qatar's National Development Strategy (NDS3) and its overarching National Vision 2030. These frameworks provide a clear roadmap for the nation's economic and social development, outlining key priorities and sectors targeted for growth.

Economic Diversification: Focus on sectors that contribute to Qatar's economic diversification efforts, reducing reliance on hydrocarbons and fostering a more balanced and resilient economy. This includes sectors such as tourism, technology, manufacturing, healthcare, and education.

Private Sector Growth: Prioritize investments that support private sector growth, recognizing its crucial role in driving innovation, job creation, and sustainable economic development. This includes investments in small and medium-sized enterprises (SMEs), entrepreneurship, and private sector-led initiatives.

Sustainability: Align investments with Qatar's commitment to sustainability, focusing on projects that promote environmental protection, resource conservation, and a transition to a low-carbon economy. This includes investments in renewable energy, energy efficiency, green buildings, and sustainable transportation.

Government Support and Incentives: By aligning with national priorities, investors can benefit from government support, incentives, and a more favourable regulatory environment. The Qatari government is actively seeking to attract foreign investment in strategic sectors, offering a range of incentives, including tax breaks, subsidized land, and streamlined approval processes.

Partnership and Collaboration:

Leveraging Local Expertise: Navigating the Qatari business environment and regulatory landscape requires a deep understanding of local customs, regulations, and business practices. Partnering with local companies or individuals with proven expertise can provide valuable insights, facilitate market entry, and enhance investment success.

Building Strong Partnerships: Establishing strong and mutually beneficial partnerships with Qatari stakeholders is crucial for long-term success. This includes partnerships with government agencies, private sector companies, academic institutions, and civil society organizations.

Knowledge Transfer: Partnerships can facilitate knowledge transfer, skills development, and technology exchange, benefiting both foreign investors and Qatari partners.

Joint Ventures: Joint ventures with Qatari companies can provide access to local markets, distribution networks, and established business relationships.

Community Engagement: Engaging with local communities and understanding their needs and priorities is essential for building sustainable and socially responsible investments. This includes supporting local initiatives, creating job opportunities for Qataris, and contributing to the nation's social development.

Long-Term Perspective:

Economic Transformation as a Journey: Qatar's economic transformation is a long-term journey, requiring a patient and strategic approach from investors. It is essential to recognize that building a diversified and sustainable economy takes time, and investors should be prepared for a long-term commitment.

Building Trust and Relationships: Developing strong relationships with Qatari stakeholders takes time and effort. Investors should focus on building trust, demonstrating a genuine commitment to Qatar's long-term development, and fostering mutually beneficial partnerships.

Adapting to Change: Qatar's economy is dynamic and evolving, and investors need to be adaptable and responsive to change. This includes staying abreast of new regulations, emerging market trends, and evolving government priorities.

In conclusion, investing in Qatar's economic transformation presents a unique opportunity for those seeking long-term growth and impact. By aligning with national priorities, embracing partnership and collaboration, and adopting a long-term perspective, investors can contribute to Qatar's sustainable development and reap the rewards of its promising future.

Chapter conclusion: Qatar: A Beacon of Economic Transformation in the Gulf

Qatar's successful hosting of the 2022 FIFA World Cup showcased its ability to execute complex projects on a global stage. However, the nation's ambitions extend far beyond sporting events. Qatar is on a remarkable journey of economic transformation, driven by a strategic vision to diversify its economy, foster sustainable growth, and create a thriving environment for businesses and investors.

The nation's commitment to diversification is evident in the robust growth of its non-hydrocarbon sectors, fuelled by substantial investments in infrastructure, tourism, and human capital development. The North Field LNG expansion project, while rooted in the hydrocarbon sector, is acting as a catalyst for broader economic growth, generating opportunities across a multitude of industries.

Qatar's fiscal prudence, underpinned by a commitment to the Permanent Income Hypothesis, ensures intergenerational equity and resilience against external shocks. The government's focus on revenue diversification, expenditure optimization, and strategic investments in key sectors lays a solid foundation for long-term economic sustainability.

The nation's stable and secure investment climate, characterized by strong macroeconomic fundamentals, a business-friendly environment, and a robust financial sector, is attracting global attention. Qatar's strategic location, coupled with its world-class infrastructure, further enhances its appeal as a hub for regional and international trade.

The IMF report identifies a wealth of opportunities for investors in Qatar's transforming economy, particularly in areas such as digitalization, renewable energy, tourism, and human capital development. Success, however, requires a strategic approach, a commitment to partnership and collaboration, and a long-term perspective.

By aligning with national priorities outlined in NDS3 and QNV 2030, leveraging local expertise, and building strong partnerships, investors can contribute to Qatar's sustainable development and reap the rewards of its promising future. Qatar's journey of economic transformation is a testament to its visionary leadership, its commitment to progress, and its determination to create a prosperous and diversified economy for generations to come.

Bahaa G. Arnouk

Oman: Embracing a Future Beyond Oil

Oman's economic landscape is undergoing a remarkable transformation, driven by the ambitious goals outlined in Oman Vision 2040. This vision sets a clear path for the Sultanate to transition from an oil-dependent economy to a diversified and sustainable one, creating a wealth of opportunities for discerning investors. This chapter, drawing insights from different sources like the International Monetary Fund's (IMF) recent Article IV Consultation report and others, delves into the exciting developments shaping the Omani market and highlights the promising prospects that lie ahead.

Beyond Oil: Charting a Course for a Diversified and Resilient Economy

While hydrocarbons have historically been the cornerstone of Oman's economy, the Sultanate is demonstrating a firm commitment to diversifying its economic base and building a more resilient future. This transition is evident in the impressive performance of non-hydrocarbon sectors, which are emerging as key drivers of economic growth.

Non-hydrocarbon growth accelerated to 2.1 percent in 2023, fuelled by a recovering agricultural and construction sector, as well as robust growth in services. This positive momentum is not a fleeting trend; it reflects a deliberate and strategic shift towards a more diversified economic model. The IMF projects this non-hydrocarbon growth to reach a steady 4 percent over the medium term, highlighting the sustainability of this transformation.

Several factors are converging to propel this impressive growth in non-hydrocarbon sectors:

- Global Demand Recovery: As the global economy recovers from recent shocks, demand for Omani exports, particularly in non-hydrocarbon sectors, is expected to increase. This will provide a boost to sectors like manufacturing, tourism, and logistics, creating jobs and stimulating economic activity.

- Structural Reforms: Oman is implementing a comprehensive suite of structural reforms aimed at enhancing competitiveness, improving the business environment, and attracting foreign investment. These reforms are creating a more level playing field for businesses, fostering innovation, and driving productivity growth. Key reforms include streamlining regulations, enhancing labor market flexibility, and promoting private sector participation in key sectors.

- Private Investment Surge: Oman is witnessing a surge in private investment, particularly in non-hydrocarbon sectors. This is being driven by a number of factors, including the government's commitment to creating a favourable investment climate, the availability of attractive investment opportunities, and growing confidence in the long-term prospects of the Omani economy. The Oman Investment Authority (OIA) is playing a key role in attracting and facilitating private investment, particularly through its strategic divestment program and its focus on developing key sectors, such as renewable energy, tourism, and logistics.

This shift towards a more diversified economy is not only enhancing Oman's resilience to oil price fluctuations but also creating a more dynamic and sustainable economic model. The growth in non-hydrocarbon sectors is creating new jobs, boosting incomes, and improving living standards for Omanis. This transformation is a testament to the government's commitment to building a brighter future for its people and positioning Oman as a leading destination for investment and economic opportunity in the region.

Navigating the Fiscal Landscape: A Prudent Path to Sustainability

Oman's steadfast commitment to fiscal discipline has been paramount, a commitment clearly reflected in the remarkable turnaround of its fiscal position. From years of deficits, Oman achieved an impressive surplus of 10.1 percent of GDP in 2022, and this fiscal prudence is projected to continue, with an estimated surplus of 5.5 percent of GDP in 2023. This achievement is a testament to the effectiveness of the government's comprehensive fiscal consolidation strategy, which has focused on three key pillars:

- Expenditure Rationalization: The government has taken decisive steps to rationalize expenditures, focusing on prioritizing essential spending, improving efficiency, and reducing waste. This has involved carefully scrutinizing spending programs, identifying areas for cost savings, and implementing measures to enhance budget transparency and accountability.

- Revenue Diversification: Recognizing the need to reduce reliance on volatile hydrocarbon revenues, Oman has embarked on a path of revenue diversification. This involves broadening the tax base, strengthening tax administration, and exploring new sources of non-hydrocarbon revenue. These efforts are not only enhancing fiscal resilience but also creating a more sustainable and balanced revenue structure for the long term.

- Prudent Debt Management: Oman has implemented a prudent debt management strategy aimed at reducing public debt levels and mitigating risks. This strategy has involved prioritizing debt repayment, optimizing debt maturity profiles, and diversifying funding sources. The government's proactive approach to debt management has significantly reduced debt vulnerabilities and enhanced investor confidence.

Looking ahead, Oman is not resting on its laurels. The government is actively pursuing further fiscal reforms to solidify these gains, build even stronger fiscal buffers, and enhance long-term fiscal sustainability. Key priorities on this reform agenda include:

Modernizing Tax Administration: Broadening the Tax Base and Enhancing Compliance

A comprehensive tax administration reform plan is underway, aimed at modernizing systems, processes, and technology to enhance efficiency, transparency, and taxpayer compliance. This reform is crucial to reducing the tax gap, broadening the tax base, and generating sustainable non-hydrocarbon revenue. Key elements of this reform plan include:

- Implementing VAT e-invoicing: The introduction of VAT e-invoicing will enhance real-time monitoring of transactions, reduce opportunities for tax evasion, and improve compliance.
- Expanding the Taxpayer Registry: Efforts are underway to expand the taxpayer registry to capture all businesses and individuals liable for taxes, further broadening the tax base.
- Simplifying Tax Filing and Payment Processes: The government is simplifying tax filing and payment processes to reduce compliance costs and encourage voluntary compliance.

In addition to strengthening tax administration, Oman is exploring the potential introduction of a personal income tax. This would mark a significant step towards diversifying government revenue streams, reducing reliance on hydrocarbon revenues, and enhancing fiscal resilience.

Phasing Out Untargeted Subsidies: Promoting Efficiency and Sustainability

Oman is committed to phasing out untargeted electricity and fuel subsidies, a move that is crucial to promoting efficient resource allocation, reducing fiscal vulnerabilities, and creating a more sustainable energy sector. This reform is being implemented gradually and strategically, with a focus on mitigating the impact on vulnerable households through targeted social safety net programs.

The government is strengthening the social safety net to protect vulnerable households from the impact of subsidy reforms. This includes expanding existing social assistance programs, introducing new targeted programs, and enhancing the effectiveness of delivery mechanisms. These measures will ensure that the benefits of subsidy reforms are shared equitably and that vulnerable households are protected from any adverse impacts.

Strengthening Fiscal Frameworks: Enhancing Transparency, Predictability, & Accountability

Oman is taking concrete steps to strengthen its fiscal frameworks, enhancing transparency, predictability, and accountability in fiscal policy. This includes:

- Strengthening the Medium-Term Fiscal Framework (MTFF): The government is strengthening its MTFF to provide a clearer and more comprehensive roadmap for fiscal policy over the medium term. This will enhance fiscal planning, improve coordination across government agencies, and provide greater certainty to investors.

- Exploring the Adoption of a Fiscal Rule: Oman is exploring the adoption of a fiscal rule to delink spending from volatile oil price fluctuations and ensure intergenerational equity. A fiscal rule would provide a clear and transparent framework for fiscal policy, enhance credibility, and promote long-term fiscal sustainability.

These efforts to strengthen fiscal frameworks are crucial to bolstering investor confidence, promoting macroeconomic stability, and ensuring that Oman's fiscal position remains strong and sustainable for generations to come.

A Magnet for Investment: Oman's Favourable Investment Climate

Oman is actively cultivating a welcoming and supportive investment climate, attracting foreign direct investment, and creating a fertile ground for businesses to thrive. The Sultanate's commitment to sound economic policies, its strategic vision for diversification, and its ongoing efforts to enhance the business environment are paying dividends. Recent upgrades in sovereign credit ratings, to just one notch below investment grade, are a testament to the growing confidence in Oman's economic prospects and its commitment to creating a sustainable and prosperous future.

Oman offers a compelling mix of attractive features for investors, making it a standout destination for those seeking growth and expansion in a stable and promising market:

Business-Friendly Reforms: Streamlining the Path to Success

Oman has embarked on a comprehensive program of business-friendly reforms, creating a more welcoming and efficient environment for businesses to operate and thrive. These reforms are focused on streamlining regulations, reducing bureaucracy, and enhancing transparency, making it easier for businesses to navigate the regulatory landscape and focus on growth.

Key reforms include:

- New Commercial Companies Law: This law simplifies the process of establishing and operating businesses in Oman, providing greater flexibility and reducing administrative burdens.
- Foreign Capital Investment Law: This law encourages foreign investment by providing a clear and transparent framework for foreign investors, guaranteeing equal treatment, and protecting their investments.
- Streamlined Licensing and Permitting Processes: Oman has streamlined licensing and permitting processes, reducing processing times and making it easier for businesses to obtain the necessary approvals to operate.
- Digitalization of Government Services: The government is actively digitalizing government services, making it easier for businesses to interact with government agencies and access information online.

These reforms, coupled with the government's ongoing commitment to improving the ease of doing business, are making Oman an increasingly attractive destination for both domestic and foreign investors.

Enhanced Social Protection: Investing in Human Capital and Social Equity

Oman's commitment to building a more inclusive and equitable society is reflected in its newly implemented social protection law. This comprehensive law provides a wide range of benefits, strengthening social safety nets and ensuring a basic level of support for all citizens. Key features of the new social protection law include:

- Universal Child Benefits: These benefits provide financial support to families with children, helping to reduce child poverty and improve child well-being.
- Disability Benefits: These benefits provide financial support to individuals with disabilities, enabling them to live with dignity and participate in society.
- Senior Citizen Benefits: These benefits provide financial support to senior citizens, ensuring their financial security and well-being in their later years.
- Harmonized Pension System: The new law harmonizes pension entitlements across public and private sectors, creating a more equitable and sustainable pension system and facilitating greater labor mobility.

These social protection measures not only enhance social equity but also contribute to a more productive and stable workforce, benefiting businesses and the economy as a whole.

Improved Governance: Transparency, Accountability, and Efficiency

Oman is committed to enhancing governance, transparency, and accountability across all sectors, creating a more predictable and reliable environment for businesses. The Oman Investment Authority (OIA) is playing a leading role in driving this transformation, particularly through its focus on improving the governance of state-owned enterprises (SOEs).

The OIA's Rawabet program is a comprehensive initiative aimed at enhancing governance, performance, and risk management within SOEs. Key elements of this program include:

- Robust Code of Governance for SOEs: This code sets clear standards for transparency, accountability, and ethical conduct within SOEs.

- Performance Assessments: Regular performance assessments are conducted to monitor the performance of SOEs and identify areas for improvement.
- Risk Management Frameworks: Comprehensive risk management frameworks have been established to identify, assess, and mitigate risks within SOEs.

The OIA is also actively pursuing a strategic divestment program, reducing the role of the state in the economy and opening up opportunities for private investors in sectors previously dominated by SOEs. This is creating a more competitive business environment, attracting foreign investment, and driving economic diversification.

A Compelling Investment Proposition

These initiatives, coupled with Oman's strategic location, abundant natural resources, and skilled workforce, create a compelling investment proposition for businesses seeking growth and expansion in a stable and promising market. Oman is a land of opportunity, and its government is committed to creating an environment where businesses can thrive and contribute to the country's sustainable development.

Key Takeaways for Investors: Navigating Oman's Transformative Journey

Oman's economic transformation under Oman Vision 2040 presents a compelling opportunity for investors seeking growth and diversification in a stable and promising market. The Sultanate is not merely tinkering with its economic model; it is embarking on a comprehensive and ambitious journey of transformation, creating a wealth of opportunities for discerning investors who understand the dynamics of this evolving landscape. Here are key takeaways to guide investors as they navigate this exciting journey:

Strategic Alignment: Capitalizing on Oman's Vision for the Future

Oman Vision 2040 is not just a policy document; it is a blueprint for the Sultanate's future, outlining a clear roadmap for economic diversification and sustainable development. Investors seeking to maximize their returns and contribute to Oman's long-term success should align their investments with the strategic sectors identified in this vision.

Key sectors poised for significant growth include:

Renewable Energy: Oman is rapidly emerging as a global leader in green hydrogen production, attracting billions of dollars in foreign investment. Investing in this burgeoning sector offers the potential for high returns while contributing to a cleaner and more sustainable energy future.

Tourism: Oman's stunning natural beauty, rich cultural heritage, and growing tourism infrastructure make it an attractive destination for tourism-related investments. Opportunities abound in hospitality, travel, leisure, and entertainment, as Oman seeks to attract a larger share of global tourism.

Logistics: Oman's strategic location and its ongoing investments in world-class logistics infrastructure are transforming the Sultanate into a regional logistics hub. Investing in logistics, transportation, and warehousing offers the potential for significant growth as Oman capitalizes on its strategic position and its growing trade links with the world.

Manufacturing: Oman is actively promoting the growth of its manufacturing sector, focusing on value-added industries that leverage local resources and expertise. Investing in manufacturing, particularly in sectors like food processing, chemicals, and building materials, offers the potential for strong returns as Oman seeks to become a regional manufacturing powerhouse.

Fisheries: Oman's rich fishing grounds and its commitment to sustainable fisheries management make it an attractive destination for fisheries-related investments. Opportunities exist in aquaculture, fish processing, and seafood exports as Oman seeks to maximize the value of its marine resources.

These strategic sectors are not only supported by government initiatives and incentives but also by a growing domestic market, a skilled workforce, and a business-friendly environment. By aligning their investments with Oman Vision 2040, investors can position themselves to capitalize on the Sultanate's long-term growth trajectory.

Partnership Opportunities: Leveraging Local Expertise and Networks

Navigating a new market can be challenging, and Oman is no exception. Building strong partnerships with local entities is crucial for investors seeking to succeed in the Omani market. Local partners can provide invaluable insights into the market, navigate the regulatory environment, and provide access to local market knowledge and networks.

Key benefits of partnering with local entities include:

Market Expertise: Local partners have a deep understanding of the Omani market, its dynamics, and its nuances. They can provide valuable insights into consumer preferences, market trends, and competitive landscape.

Regulatory Guidance: Navigating the regulatory environment in a new market can be complex and time-consuming. Local partners can help investors understand and comply with local regulations, ensuring a smooth and efficient entry into the market.

Network Access: Local partners have established networks and relationships with key stakeholders, including government agencies, business associations, and potential customers. This can open doors for investors and facilitate business development.

Building strong partnerships with local entities can significantly enhance investors' chances of success in the Omani market, mitigating risks and maximizing returns.

Long-Term Perspective: Investing in a Sustainable Future

Oman's economic transformation is a long-term endeavour, and investors should adopt a patient and strategic approach to investment. Short-term gains should not be prioritized over long-term sustainability. Investors should focus on building businesses that contribute to Oman's long-term development goals, creating value for both their stakeholders and the Omani people.

Key considerations for long-term investment in Oman include:

- **Sustainability**: Invest in businesses that are environmentally and socially responsible, contributing to Oman's sustainable development goals.
- **Job Creation**: Prioritize investments that create jobs for Omanis, contributing to the development of a skilled and productive workforce.
- **Knowledge Transfer**: Seek opportunities to transfer knowledge and expertise to Omani partners, contributing to the development of local capacity.

By adopting a long-term perspective and focusing on building sustainable businesses, investors can create lasting value, contribute to Oman's economic transformation, and strengthen their own reputation as responsible and impactful investors.

Seizing the Opportunity: A New Dawn for Investment in Oman

Oman's economic transformation presents a compelling opportunity for investors who are seeking growth and diversification in a stable and promising market. The Sultanate is laying the groundwork for a prosperous future, one that is built on a diversified economy, a strong commitment to sustainability, and a welcoming environment for foreign investment. By aligning their investments with Oman Vision 2040, building strong partnerships with local entities, and adopting a long-term perspective, investors can position themselves to capitalize on the exciting opportunities emerging in Oman's dynamic and evolving economy. The message is clear: Oman is open for business, and the time to invest is now.

Chapter conclusion: Oman's Transformation: An Opportunity for Discerning Investors

This chapter has painted a compelling picture of Oman's ongoing economic transformation, driven by the ambitious goals of Oman Vision 2040. The Sultanate is resolutely moving away from its dependence on hydrocarbons, charting a course towards a diversified, sustainable, and resilient economy. This strategic shift is evident in the impressive growth of non-hydrocarbon sectors, fuelled by global demand recovery, comprehensive structural reforms, and a surge in private investment.

Oman's commitment to fiscal discipline is equally commendable. The remarkable turnaround from years of deficits to consecutive surpluses demonstrates the effectiveness of the government's fiscal consolidation strategy. Furthermore, the government is actively pursuing additional reforms to modernize tax administration, phase out untargeted subsidies, and strengthen fiscal frameworks, ensuring long-term fiscal sustainability and enhancing investor confidence.

Creating a welcoming investment climate is a cornerstone of Oman's strategy for attracting foreign direct investment and driving economic growth. The Sultanate is implementing business-friendly reforms, strengthening social protection, and improving governance, creating a fertile ground for businesses to thrive. These initiatives, coupled with Oman's strategic location, abundant natural resources, and skilled workforce, make it a highly attractive destination for investors seeking growth and diversification in a stable and promising market.

For investors, the key takeaway is clear: Oman is a land of opportunity. By aligning their investments with the strategic sectors outlined in Oman Vision 2040, forging strong partnerships with local entities, and adopting a long-term perspective, investors can capitalize on the Sultanate's transformative journey and contribute to its sustainable development while reaping significant rewards. The time to invest in Oman is now, as the Sultanate embarks on a new dawn of economic prosperity.

Bahaa G. Arnouk

UAE: the UAE's Financial System: A Rock of Stability in Uncertain Times

The United Arab Emirates (UAE) is rapidly emerging as a global economic powerhouse, driven by its ambitious diversification strategy and commitment to sustainable growth. This chapter, drawing insights from different sources including the International Monetary Fund's (IMF) June 2023 Article IV Consultation report, explores the UAE's economic landscape, highlighting both challenges and opportunities for investors.

Beyond Oil: A Diversification Success Story

While oil remains a significant contributor to the UAE's economy, the nation has embarked on a successful journey of diversification. This strategic shift is evident in the projected non-hydrocarbon GDP growth, which is expected to reach 3.8% in 2023. This robust growth is fuelled by several key factors:

Robust Domestic Activity: The UAE's domestic economy is thriving, driven by a resurgence in consumer spending and business investment. This is particularly noticeable in sectors like retail, hospitality, and real estate.

Tourism Rebound: The tourism sector has witnessed a remarkable recovery following the pandemic, exceeding expectations. This rebound is attributed to the successful hosting of the Dubai World Expo, which attracted millions of visitors and showcased the UAE's capabilities on a global stage. Additionally, the FIFA World Cup in neighbouring Qatar has generated positive spillovers for the UAE's tourism industry.

Capital Expenditure: The UAE government continues to invest heavily in infrastructure projects, including transportation, logistics, and renewable energy. These investments not only create jobs and stimulate economic activity but also enhance the UAE's attractiveness as a global business hub.

UAE's 2050 Strategies: The UAE's long-term vision, encapsulated in its 2050 strategies, provides a roadmap for sustainable and diversified growth. These strategies prioritize key sectors like trade, digitalization, and green initiatives, attracting foreign investment and fostering innovation.

The IMF projects this non-hydrocarbon growth to continue in the medium term, underpinned by these strategic initiatives.

Manufacturing: A Key Driver of Future Growth

The manufacturing sector is poised for significant expansion in the medium term, driven by both hydrocarbon and non-hydrocarbon related industries. The UAE's focus on developing downstream industries in the hydrocarbon sector, such as petrochemicals and refining, is creating new opportunities for manufacturing. Additionally, the growth of non-hydrocarbon sectors like renewable energy, aerospace, and advanced technology is further boosting demand for manufacturing activities.

Key Initiatives Supporting Diversification:

Comprehensive Economic Partnership Agreements (CEPAs): The UAE is actively pursuing CEPAs with key trading partners worldwide. These agreements aim to reduce trade barriers, boost exports, and attract foreign investment, further diversifying the economy and integrating the UAE into global value chains.

Digitalization: The UAE is investing heavily in digital infrastructure and technologies, including artificial intelligence, blockchain, and cloud computing. This digital transformation is creating new opportunities for businesses across various sectors, from e-commerce and fintech to healthcare and education.

Green Initiatives: The UAE is committed to achieving net-zero emissions by 2050, investing in renewable energy, green finance, and sustainable infrastructure. This commitment not only contributes to global sustainability efforts but also creates new economic opportunities in green technologies and industries.

The UAE's commitment to diversification is evident in its proactive policies and strategic investments. This transformation is not only reducing the nation's reliance on oil but also positioning it as a global leader in innovation, sustainability, and economic dynamism.

A Hub for Innovation and Investment

The UAE has strategically positioned itself as a global magnet for innovation and investment, attracting significant attention from international businesses and investors. This success is driven by a confluence of factors:

Business-Friendly Reforms: The UAE government has implemented a series of business-friendly reforms, streamlining regulations, reducing bureaucratic hurdles, and creating a more conducive environment for investment. These reforms have significantly improved the ease of doing business in the UAE, making it a more attractive destination for foreign companies.

Strategic Location: Situated at the crossroads of Europe, Asia, and Africa, the UAE enjoys a strategic geographical advantage. This prime location provides businesses with unparalleled access to key markets and trade routes, making it an ideal hub for regional and global operations.

World-Class Infrastructure: The UAE boasts world-class infrastructure, including modern airports, seaports, telecommunications networks, and transportation systems. This robust infrastructure facilitates seamless business operations, logistics, and connectivity, further enhancing the UAE's appeal to investors.

Innovation Ecosystem: The UAE is actively fostering an innovation ecosystem, investing heavily in research and development, technology incubators, and start-up support programs. This focus on innovation is attracting entrepreneurs, tech companies, and investors seeking to capitalize on the UAE's dynamic and forward-looking environment.

Digital and Green Technologies: The UAE is at the forefront of adopting and investing in digital and green technologies. This includes significant investments in artificial intelligence, blockchain, renewable energy, and sustainable infrastructure. These investments not only contribute to the UAE's economic diversification but also position it as a leader in the global transition towards a more sustainable future.

The IMF report underscores the UAE's remarkable success in attracting safe-haven inflows and conducting major Initial Public Offerings (IPOs), even amidst heightened global uncertainty. This highlights the strong confidence investors have in the UAE's economic resilience, stability, and long-term growth prospects.

Attracting Safe-Haven Inflows:

The UAE has emerged as a safe haven for investors seeking stability and security during times of global economic turbulence. This is due to several factors, including:

Stable Political Environment: The UAE enjoys a stable political environment, providing investors with a sense of security and predictability.

Strong Economic Fundamentals: The UAE's strong economic fundamentals, including a diversified economy, robust fiscal position, and well-regulated financial system, make it a reliable and attractive destination for investment.

Currency Peg to the US Dollar: The UAE dirham's peg to the US dollar provides currency stability, reducing exchange rate risks for investors.

Successful IPOs:

The UAE has witnessed a surge in successful IPOs in recent years, attracting significant capital from both domestic and international investors. This success is attributed to:

Growing Investor Confidence: The UAE's strong economic performance, business-friendly environment, and commitment to innovation have boosted investor confidence, making IPOs more attractive.

Supportive Regulatory Framework: The UAE has a well-regulated and transparent capital market, providing a conducive environment for IPOs.

Strong Demand from Institutional Investors: The UAE's IPOs have attracted strong demand from institutional investors, both locally and globally, seeking to capitalize on the UAE's growth potential.

The UAE's success in attracting investment and fostering innovation is a testament to its strategic vision, proactive policies, and commitment to creating a sustainable and prosperous future. This makes the UAE a compelling destination for businesses and investors seeking to capitalize on the opportunities presented by a dynamic and rapidly evolving global economy.

Navigating the Fiscal Landscape

The UAE's fiscal landscape is currently characterized by strength and stability, a testament to its prudent fiscal management and the windfall from elevated oil prices. The IMF report acknowledges this strong fiscal position, projecting large surpluses in the coming years. The general government fiscal balance is expected to average a healthy 3.8 percent of GDP over the medium term. This positive outlook is further reinforced by the UAE's commitment to maintaining a prudent fiscal stance, evident in its successful issuance of USD 7 billion in international bonds and AED 9 billion in domestic bonds, demonstrating strong investor confidence in the UAE's economic future.

However, further solidifying this fiscal position to ensure long-term sustainability and resilience is required, particularly in the face of potential future oil price volatility and the global transition towards a lower-carbon economy. The IMF staff consultation report on UAE 2023 outlines key recommendations for achieving this:

Maintaining a Prudent Fiscal Stance:

Avoiding Procyclical Spending: The UAE should resist the temptation to increase spending excessively during periods of high oil revenues. Instead, it should prioritize saving a significant portion of these windfalls to build fiscal buffers, providing a cushion against future economic shocks or declines in oil prices.

Building Fiscal Buffers: Accumulating fiscal reserves during periods of economic prosperity is crucial for enhancing medium-term sustainability. These reserves can be utilized to counter economic downturns, finance strategic investments, or support social safety nets during challenging times.

Broadening the Revenue Base:

Enhancing Non-Hydrocarbon Revenue: Reducing reliance on oil revenue is crucial for long-term fiscal sustainability. The UAE should continue to diversify its revenue sources by expanding its non-hydrocarbon revenue base. This can be achieved through measures such as:

Introducing New Taxes: The newly introduced corporate income tax (CIT) is a significant step towards broadening the tax base and is expected to improve the adjusted non-hydrocarbon primary deficit by 2.2 percentage points to 20.4 percent of non-hydrocarbon GDP over 2023-2027.

Expanding the Tax Base: Exploring other potential tax avenues, such as property taxes or value-added taxes, could further enhance non-hydrocarbon revenue.

Improving Tax Collection Efficiency: Strengthening tax administration, leveraging technology, and addressing tax evasion can significantly improve revenue collection.

Improving Expenditure Efficiency:

Gradual Phase-Out of Subsidies: While subsidies can provide social benefits, they can also strain government finances and distort market mechanisms. The UAE should implement a gradual and well-communicated phase-out of subsidies, accompanied by targeted measures to mitigate the impact on vulnerable households.

Strengthening Social Safety Nets: As subsidies are phased out, it is crucial to strengthen social safety nets to protect vulnerable populations from potential economic hardship. This includes expanding social assistance programs, improving access to healthcare and education, and providing targeted support for low-income households.

Growth-Friendly Consolidation: The IMF suggests a growth-friendly and credible medium-term average annual consolidation of the non-hydrocarbon primary fiscal deficit of around 0.4 percent of non-hydrocarbon GDP. This gradual consolidation approach aims to balance fiscal sustainability with continued economic growth and development.

Further Strengthening Public Finances:

The IMF report also recommends additional measures to further strengthen public finances:

Broadening the Tax Base: Continuously exploring opportunities to expand the tax base, including through the introduction of new taxes or broadening the scope of existing ones, can enhance revenue generation.

Improving Tax Collection Efficiency: Implementing measures to improve tax compliance, streamline tax administration, and leverage technology can significantly enhance revenue collection.

Containing Expenditure Growth: Maintaining strict control over government spending, prioritizing essential expenditures, and improving efficiency in public service delivery can help contain expenditure growth.

Gradually Phasing Out Subsidies: Continuing the gradual phase-out of subsidies, while ensuring targeted support for vulnerable groups, can reduce fiscal burdens and promote market efficiency.

By implementing these recommendations, the UAE can ensure fiscal sustainability, enhance its resilience to economic shocks, and support its long-term economic goals, including its ambitious diversification strategy and transition towards a more sustainable future. This proactive approach to fiscal management will not only strengthen the UAE's economic foundation but also reinforce its position as a global leader in economic stability and resilience.

A Secure and Stable Financial System

The UAE's financial system stands as a pillar of strength, characterized by its overall stability and resilience. This financial soundness is further reinforced by the Central Bank of the UAE's (CBUAE) proactive approach to monitoring and mitigating financial stability risks. The report also notes the banking sector's improved profitability, driven by higher interest income resulting from rising interest rates and steady growth in private credit.

However, the report acknowledges the persistence of certain vulnerabilities within the financial system, particularly exposures to the real estate sector. To further enhance the robustness and attractiveness of the UAE's financial system to investors, several key measures are recommended:

Strengthening Macroprudential Frameworks:

Effective Supervision of Digital Innovation and Fintech Activities: The rapid rise of digital innovation and fintech presents both opportunities and challenges for the financial sector. The UAE needs to ensure effective supervision of these activities to mitigate potential risks while fostering innovation. This includes:

- Developing robust regulatory frameworks for fintech companies, addressing issues such as data privacy, cybersecurity, and consumer protection.
- Enhancing the CBUAE's supervisory capacity to effectively monitor and regulate fintech activities.
- Promoting responsible innovation in the financial sector, encouraging the development of fintech solutions that benefit consumers and businesses while maintaining financial stability.

Continued Monitoring of Financial Stability Risks: The IMF recommends continuous and vigilant monitoring of financial stability risks, particularly in light of:

- High Level of Nonperforming Loans (NPLs): While NPLs have decreased from their pandemic peak, they remain elevated compared to historical levels. The CBUAE should continue to monitor NPL trends, encourage banks to effectively manage and reduce NPLs, and ensure adequate provisioning.

- Tightening Financial Conditions: Rising interest rates and global economic uncertainty can create challenges for borrowers, potentially leading to increased NPLs and financial stress. The CBUAE should closely monitor these developments and implement appropriate macroprudential measures to mitigate risks.
- Banks' Exposures to Real Estate: The real estate sector remains a key area of vulnerability. The CBUAE should continue to monitor banks' exposures to real estate, ensure compliance with existing prudential regulations, and consider additional measures to mitigate risks if necessary.

Strengthening the AML/CFT Framework:

Addressing Remaining Deficiencies: significant progress was made by the UAE in strengthening its Anti-Money Laundering and Combating the Financing of Terrorism (AML/CFT) framework under the National AML/CFT Strategy and Action Plan. However, continued efforts are urged to address remaining deficiencies identified by the Financial Action Task Force (FATF). This includes:

- Enhancing beneficial ownership transparency to prevent the misuse of corporate structures for illicit activities.
- Strengthening the CBUAE's supervisory capacity to effectively monitor and enforce AML/CFT regulations.
- Enhancing international cooperation in AML/CFT matters to combat cross-border financial crimes.

Additional Recommendations:

The IMF report also suggests several additional measures to further strengthen the UAE's financial sector:

- Promoting Effective Management of Legacy NPLs: The CBUAE should encourage banks to actively manage and reduce legacy NPLs through measures such as loan restructuring, asset sales, or write-offs, while ensuring adequate provisioning.

- Further Strengthening Regulation and Supervision of the Insurance Sector: The insurance sector plays a crucial role in financial stability. The UAE should continue to strengthen regulation and supervision of the insurance sector to ensure its soundness and resilience.
- Carefully Balancing Opportunities and Risks Associated with Digital Innovation: While embracing digital innovation, the UAE should carefully assess and mitigate potential risks associated with new technologies and business models in the banking and payments sector. This includes ensuring cybersecurity, data privacy, and consumer protection.

By implementing these recommendations, the UAE can further enhance the robustness and attractiveness of its financial system, attracting more investment, fostering innovation, and solidifying its position as a leading global financial centre. This proactive approach to strengthening the financial sector will not only contribute to the UAE's economic growth and stability but also enhance its reputation as a safe and reliable destination for international investors and businesses.

Opportunities Amidst Transformation

The UAE is undergoing a remarkable economic transformation, driven by its ambitious diversification strategy, commitment to innovation, and focus on sustainability. Several key areas ripe for investment can be identified, presenting lucrative opportunities for businesses and investors seeking to capitalize on the UAE's dynamic growth trajectory:

Digitalization: A Catalyst for Growth and Diversification

The UAE is investing heavily in building a robust digital infrastructure and embracing cutting-edge technologies, creating a fertile ground for businesses operating in the digital sphere. This digital transformation is opening up a plethora of opportunities in various sectors:

E-commerce: The UAE's e-commerce market is experiencing exponential growth, driven by high internet and smartphone penetration, a young and tech-savvy population, and a growing preference for online shopping. This presents significant opportunities for e-commerce platforms, online retailers, and logistics providers.

Fintech: The UAE is rapidly becoming a regional fintech hub, attracting innovative startups and established financial institutions alike. The government's supportive regulatory environment, coupled with a strong demand for digital financial services, is driving growth in areas such as mobile payments, digital banking, and blockchain technology.

Artificial Intelligence (AI): The UAE is positioning itself as a global leader in AI, investing in research and development, talent acquisition, and the development of AI-powered solutions across various sectors, including healthcare, education, transportation, and government services.

The transformative potential of AI and digitalization is huge and urging continued investments to enable infrastructure to support economic diversification and facilitate a smooth energy transition.

Green Initiatives: Pioneering a Sustainable Future

The UAE is demonstrating a strong commitment to sustainability, setting ambitious targets to achieve net-zero emissions by 2050. This commitment is translating into significant investments and opportunities in the green sector:

Renewable Energy: The UAE is investing heavily in renewable energy sources, particularly solar power. The country boasts some of the world's largest and most cost-effective solar projects, positioning it as a leader in the global transition towards clean energy.

Green Finance: The UAE is actively developing its green finance capabilities, promoting sustainable investments and financing mechanisms for green projects. This includes the issuance of green bonds, the establishment of green banks, and the development of sustainable finance regulations.

Sustainable Infrastructure: The UAE is prioritizing the development of sustainable infrastructure, incorporating green building standards, energy-efficient designs, and eco-friendly materials in its construction projects. This focus on sustainability is creating opportunities for companies specializing in green building technologies, sustainable construction materials, and energy-efficient solutions.

The IMF report highlights the importance of a balanced approach to energy transition, advocating for a scaling up of investments in renewable and clean energy while simultaneously "greening" extraction processes in the hydrocarbon sector. This balanced approach aims to ensure energy security while mitigating environmental impact and promoting sustainable development.

Trade and Tourism: Expanding Global Reach

The UAE is strategically expanding its trade partnerships and developing world-class tourism destinations, creating a wealth of opportunities for businesses in related sectors:

Trade: The UAE is actively pursuing Comprehensive Economic Partnership Agreements (CEPAs) with key trading partners worldwide. These agreements aim to reduce trade barriers, boost exports, and attract foreign investment, further diversifying the economy and integrating the UAE into global value chains. The IMF welcomes the UAE's progress on CEPAs, recognizing their potential to enhance trade, attract FDI, and boost the UAE's integration into global value chains.

Tourism: The UAE is renowned for its world-class tourism destinations, attracting millions of visitors annually. The country is continuously investing in developing new attractions, enhancing its hospitality infrastructure, and offering diverse tourism experiences. This creates significant opportunities for businesses in the hospitality, travel, and leisure sectors.

The UAE's strategic focus on expanding its trade partnerships and developing its tourism industry is further strengthening its position as a global hub for business and leisure, attracting investment, creating jobs, and driving economic growth.

The UAE's economic transformation presents a compelling landscape of opportunities for investors and businesses. By capitalizing on these opportunities, particularly in the areas of digitalization, green initiatives, and trade and tourism, investors can contribute to the UAE's continued economic success while reaping the rewards of its dynamic and growing market.

Key Takeaways for Investors: Navigating the UAE's Dynamic Landscape

The UAE's economic transformation presents a compelling landscape of opportunities for investors. However, navigating this dynamic environment requires a strategic approach, a long-term vision, and a thorough understanding of both the potential rewards and inherent risks. Insights for investors seeking to capitalize on the UAE's growth trajectory are:

Strategic Partnerships: The Power of Local Expertise

Collaborating with local partners is crucial for investors seeking to successfully navigate the UAE's business environment. Local partners offer invaluable advantages:

Regulatory Expertise: Navigating the UAE's regulatory landscape can be complex. Local partners possess in-depth knowledge of local laws, regulations, and business practices, helping investors avoid potential pitfalls and ensure compliance.

Market Insights: Local partners provide crucial insights into market dynamics, consumer preferences, and competitive landscapes, enabling investors to make informed decisions and tailor their strategies accordingly.

Network Access: Local partners have established networks and relationships with key stakeholders, including government officials, business leaders, and potential customers, facilitating access to opportunities and resources.

Cultural Understanding: Understanding the UAE's cultural nuances is essential for building successful business relationships. Local partners can bridge cultural gaps, ensuring effective communication and fostering trust.

Long-Term Vision: Aligning with the UAE's 2050 Strategies

Investors should adopt a long-term perspective, focusing on projects that align with the UAE's 2050 strategies. These strategies prioritize:

Economic Diversification: The UAE is actively reducing its reliance on oil, investing in sectors like tourism, logistics, manufacturing, technology, and renewable energy. Projects aligned with these diversification efforts are likely to receive government support and benefit from long-term growth prospects.

Private Sector Growth: The UAE recognizes the crucial role of the private sector in driving economic growth and innovation. Projects that contribute to private sector development, job creation, and entrepreneurship are highly encouraged.

Sustainability: The UAE is committed to sustainable development, investing in green technologies, renewable energy, and sustainable infrastructure. Projects that promote environmental sustainability and contribute to the UAE's net-zero emissions target are well-positioned for success.

Due Diligence: Assessing Risks and Opportunities

Thorough due diligence is paramount for investors to make informed decisions and mitigate potential risks. The IMF report acknowledges significant global uncertainties surrounding the UAE's outlook, including:

- **Weaker Global Growth**: A global economic slowdown could impact the UAE's growth prospects, particularly in sectors like tourism, trade, and investment. Investors should assess the potential impact of global economic headwinds on their projects and develop contingency plans.

- **Tighter Financial Conditions**: Rising interest rates and global financial market volatility can increase borrowing costs and reduce access to capital. Investors should carefully evaluate their financing options and ensure they have sufficient capital reserves to weather potential financial challenges.

- **Geopolitical Developments**: Regional and global geopolitical tensions can create uncertainty and impact investor sentiment. Investors should monitor geopolitical developments and assess their potential implications for their investments.

- **Energy Transition**: The global shift towards a lower-carbon economy presents both risks and opportunities for the UAE. Investors should carefully evaluate the potential impact of the energy transition on their projects, considering both the risks associated with declining oil demand and the opportunities presented by the growing renewable energy sector.

Chapter conclusion: The UAE's Financial System: A Beacon of Stability and Opportunity in Uncertain Times

This chapter has explored the UAE's dynamic economic landscape. The UAE's journey of transformation, driven by its ambitious diversification strategy and commitment to sustainable growth, presents a compelling narrative of resilience, innovation, and opportunity.

The nation's success in navigating the post-pandemic recovery, attracting safe-haven inflows, and conducting major IPOs amidst global uncertainty underscores its robust economic fundamentals and investor confidence. The UAE's proactive approach to fiscal management, characterized by a prudent fiscal stance, efforts to broaden the revenue base, and improve expenditure efficiency, further strengthens its economic foundation.

The UAE's financial system, marked by its stability and resilience, continues to evolve, embracing digital innovation while addressing vulnerabilities, particularly in the real estate sector. The ongoing strengthening of macroprudential frameworks and the AML/CFT regime further enhances the UAE's attractiveness as a global financial hub.

The UAE's economic transformation presents a wealth of opportunities for investors, particularly in the burgeoning fields of digitalization, green initiatives, and trade and tourism. However, navigating this dynamic landscape requires a strategic approach. Investors must forge strategic partnerships with local entities to leverage their expertise, adopt a long-term vision aligned with the UAE's 2050 strategies, and conduct thorough due diligence to assess potential risks and opportunities, particularly those stemming from global economic shifts and the energy transition.

The UAE's commitment to diversification, innovation, and sustainability positions it as a beacon of economic progress in an increasingly uncertain world. By embracing a strategic and informed approach, investors can contribute to the UAE's continued success while reaping the rewards of its dynamic and growing market.

Bahaa G. Arnouk

Kuwait: Navigating Economic Winds Amidst Abundant Wealth

Kuwait, a nation blessed with abundant oil wealth, faces a critical juncture in its economic journey. While high oil prices have fuelled a robust recovery and impressive fiscal and external balances, the country must confront persistent structural challenges to secure a prosperous and sustainable future. This chapter , drawing insights from different sources including the International Monetary Fund's (IMF) September 2023 Article IV Consultation report, explores the economic landscape of Kuwait, highlighting both its strengths and the pressing need for reforms.

Beyond the Black Gold: A Story of Resilience and Challenges

Kuwait's economic narrative is deeply intertwined with oil, a resource that has shaped its destiny for decades. While the black gold has fuelled impressive wealth and economic growth, it has also created a dependence that poses significant challenges for the country's long-term prosperity.

Non-Oil Sector: Showing Resilience, But Facing Headwinds

The non-oil sector, while demonstrating resilience in recent years, faces a number of headwinds. Growth reached an estimated 3.4 percent in 2021, driven by a recovery in domestic and external demand following the pandemic-induced contraction. This momentum continued in 2022, with non-oil GDP growth strengthening to 4.0 percent, fuelled by continued recovery in external demand and a smaller fiscal drag. This resilience is a testament to the underlying strength of the Kuwaiti economy and the government's commitment to supporting non-oil sectors.

However, the IMF report emphasizes that this growth is not sufficient to meet the needs of a rapidly growing and young Kuwaiti population. With roughly 100,000 young Kuwaitis expected to enter the workforce over the next five years, the non-oil sector needs to expand significantly to create adequate job opportunities. This demographic pressure, coupled with the global shift towards decarbonization and the long-term decline in oil revenues, makes economic diversification an urgent imperative for Kuwait.

The Urgency of Economic Diversification

There is a critical need for Kuwait to accelerate and broaden its economic diversification efforts. This means moving beyond the traditional reliance on oil and developing a more vibrant and dynamic private sector that can create high-quality jobs and drive sustainable growth. Several factors highlight the urgency of this diversification:

Diminishing Oil Revenues: The global transition towards renewable energy sources and the long-term decline in oil demand will inevitably impact Kuwait's oil revenues, making it crucial to develop alternative sources of income.

Job Creation for a Young Workforce: The large influx of young Kuwaitis entering the workforce necessitates the creation of a significant number of new jobs, which the public sector alone cannot absorb.

Enhancing Competitiveness: Kuwait's competitiveness has been declining in recent years, partly due to high labor costs and low productivity. Diversification into higher value-added sectors can help boost competitiveness and attract foreign investment.

Unlocking Kuwait's Potential

Despite the challenges, Kuwait possesses significant strengths that can be leveraged to achieve successful economic diversification. These include:

Abundant Financial Resources: Kuwait's sovereign wealth fund, one of the largest in the world, provides substantial financial resources that can be strategically deployed to support diversification efforts.

A Well-Educated Population: Kuwait boasts a highly educated population, which can be a valuable asset in developing a knowledge-based economy.

Strategic Location: Kuwait's strategic location at the heart of the Gulf region offers access to a large and growing market.

By addressing the structural bottlenecks, investing in human capital, and fostering a more dynamic and competitive private sector, Kuwait can unlock its full potential and create a more diversified and sustainable economy that can thrive in the post-oil era.

Navigating Fiscal Currents: Balancing Short-Term Needs and Long-Term Sustainability

Kuwait's fiscal position has experienced a remarkable turnaround in recent years, transitioning from a period of deficits to a period of substantial surpluses. This fiscal strengthening is largely attributed to the surge in oil revenues, coupled with a degree of expenditure restraint. The overall fiscal balance turned into a surplus of 6.5 percent of GDP in FY2021/22, and the IMF report estimates further improvement to 23.4 percent of GDP in FY2022/23. However, this positive fiscal picture masks underlying vulnerabilities that require careful navigation to ensure long-term sustainability and intergenerational equity.

The Illusion of Abundance: The Need for Fiscal Prudence

While the current fiscal surpluses might create an illusion of abundance, the IMF report cautions against complacency. The heavy reliance on volatile oil revenues makes Kuwait's fiscal position susceptible to global oil price fluctuations. Moreover, the current spending structure, characterized by a large public sector wage bill and generous energy subsidies, is not sustainable in the long run.

Charting a Sustainable Course: IMF's Recommendations

The fiscal consolidation is paramount to reinforce long-term sustainability and intergenerational equity. This means building fiscal buffers during periods of high oil prices to cushion against future shocks and ensuring that current spending does not compromise the well-being of future generations.

A growth-friendly fiscal consolidation scenario that balances the need for fiscal prudence with the objective of supporting economic growth and diversification is recommended. This scenario encompasses both revenue and expenditure measures, with a focus on:

Revenue Enhancement: Implementing a GCC-wide VAT and Excises: Introducing a VAT and excises on tobacco and sugary drinks, in line with agreements among GCC countries, would provide a stable source of non-oil revenue.

Expanding Corporate Income Taxation: Broadening the corporate income tax base to include domestic companies would enhance revenue collection and create a more level playing field for businesses.

Enhancing Revenue Administration Capacity: Strengthening the capacity of the Ministry of Finance to collect taxes and manage revenues efficiently is crucial to maximizing revenue potential.

Expenditure Rationalization:

Curtailing the Wage Bill: Containing public sector wage growth and aligning public sector wages with those in the private sector would reduce fiscal pressures and encourage private sector employment.

Gradually Phasing Out Untargeted Energy Subsidies: Phasing out energy subsidies, while providing targeted support to vulnerable households, would reduce fiscal costs, promote efficient energy consumption, and free up resources for more productive spending.

Improving the Efficiency of Capital Spending: Enhancing project planning, selection, and execution processes would ensure that capital spending is directed towards projects with high economic returns.

Beyond Fiscal Measures: The Imperative of Structural Reforms:

Fiscal consolidation alone is not sufficient to address Kuwait's economic challenges. Deep-rooted structural reforms are essential to unlock private sector-led growth and achieve sustainable economic diversification. Key areas requiring reform include per the IMF are:

Labor Market Segmentation:

- Addressing Wage Disparities: Reducing the wage gap between nationals and expatriates is crucial to incentivize private sector employment for Kuwaitis.
- Promoting Labor Market Flexibility: Introducing greater flexibility in hiring and firing workers would enhance labor market efficiency and encourage private sector job creation.

Declining Competitiveness:

- Boosting Productivity: Investing in education, training, and innovation is crucial to raising productivity and enhancing competitiveness.
- Promoting a Level Playing Field: Ensuring fair competition and reducing bureaucratic hurdles for businesses would create a more conducive environment for private sector development.

Business Environment Bottlenecks:

- Reforming Land Allocation Procedures: Introducing market-based and transparent mechanisms for land allocation would improve efficiency and attract investment.
- Easing Restrictions on Foreign Ownership: Relaxing restrictions on foreign ownership in certain sectors would attract foreign investment and promote competition.

A Comprehensive Reform Package: Charting a New Economic Course for Kuwait

Kuwait's future prosperity hinges on its ability to move beyond its dependence on oil and embrace a new economic model driven by a dynamic and competitive private sector. Achieving this vision requires a comprehensive reform package that tackles the deep-rooted structural challenges hindering the country's economic potential. The IMF report outlines a roadmap for this transformation, emphasizing four key pillars:

Labor Market Reforms: Unleashing the Power of Human Capital

Kuwait's labor market is characterized by a stark segmentation between the public and private sectors. The public sector, offering high wages, generous benefits, and job security, has attracted a disproportionate share of Kuwaiti nationals, leaving the private sector underdeveloped and reliant on expatriate labor. This imbalance has created several challenges:

Crowding Out Private Sector Development: The dominance of the public sector limits opportunities for private sector growth and job creation.

Wage Disparities and Labor Misallocation: The wage gap between nationals and expatriates discourages private sector employment for Kuwaitis and leads to a misallocation of human capital.

Low Productivity: The lack of competition and performance-based incentives in the public sector has contributed to lower productivity levels.

To address these challenges, a comprehensive set of labor market reforms are recommended including:

Aligning Public and Private Sector Wage Structures: Gradually aligning public sector wages with those in the private sector would reduce wage disparities and encourage private sector employment for Kuwaitis.

Promoting Flexibility in Hiring and Firing Workers: Introducing greater flexibility in hiring and firing practices would enhance labor market efficiency and allow businesses to adjust their workforce based on market demands.

Adopting More Flexible Labor Market Policies for Expatriates: Relaxing restrictions on expatriate labor, such as visa requirements and sponsorship rules, would attract skilled workers and enhance the competitiveness of the private sector.

Social Safety Net Enhancement: Supporting Workers During the Transition

Labor market reforms can be disruptive in the short term, potentially leading to job displacement and income loss for some workers. To mitigate these risks and ensure a smooth transition, the IMF report emphasizes the need to strengthen social safety nets:

Streamlining and Enhancing Efficiency: Improving the targeting and efficiency of social assistance programs, such as unemployment benefits and job training programs, would provide crucial support to workers during the transition.

Investing in Skills Development: Expanding vocational training programs and providing opportunities for skills upgrading would equip workers with the skills needed for a diversified economy.

Promoting Active Labor Market Policies: Strengthening job search assistance and providing incentives for private sector employment would facilitate the reintegration of displaced workers into the labor market.

Business Environment Improvements: Creating a Conducive Environment for Investment

Kuwait faces several challenges in its business environment that hinder private sector development. These include bureaucratic hurdles, restrictions on foreign ownership, and a lack of competition in certain sectors. The IMF report recommends a range of reforms to address these bottlenecks:

Streamlining Business Procedures: Simplifying and digitizing business registration, licensing, and permitting processes would reduce administrative burdens and encourage entrepreneurship.

Relaxing Restrictions on Foreign Ownership: Easing restrictions on foreign ownership in certain sectors would attract foreign investment, promote competition, and transfer knowledge and technology.

Improving Land Allocation Mechanisms: Introducing market-based and transparent mechanisms for land allocation would improve efficiency and ensure that land is allocated to its most productive uses.

Strengthening Competition Policy: Enhancing the enforcement of competition laws and promoting a level playing field for businesses would encourage innovation and efficiency.

Investment in Human Capital: Building a Knowledge-Based Economy

Kuwait boasts a high level of education attainment, but the quality of education and the relevance of skills to the needs of the private sector remain areas for improvement. Investing in human capital is vital to build a knowledge-based economy:

Enhancing Education Quality: Improving the quality of education at all levels, from primary to tertiary, is crucial to developing a skilled and adaptable workforce.

Expanding Vocational Training: Expanding access to vocational training programs would provide students with practical skills relevant to the needs of the private sector.

Fostering Research and Innovation: Investing in research and development and promoting collaboration between universities and businesses would drive innovation and create a more knowledge-intensive economy.

A long-term vision for sustainable prosperity is what Kuwait needs, implementing this comprehensive reform package will require a sustained and coordinated effort from the government, the private sector, and civil society. It will also require a long-term vision that prioritizes sustainable and inclusive growth over short-term gains. By embracing this transformative agenda, Kuwait can unlock its full economic potential and create a more prosperous and resilient future for its citizens.

Navigating the investment landscape of Kuwait

Several investment opportunities arising from Kuwait's economic landscape and its reform agenda can be highlighted. Savvy investors can leverage these insights to identify promising areas for investment and contribute to Kuwait's economic transformation. Here are some key investment opportunities:

Digitalization and Technology:

Fintech: Kuwait's robust and well-capitalized banking sector, coupled with a growing young population comfortable with technology, presents a fertile ground for fintech innovations. Opportunities exist in areas like mobile payments, digital banking, and online lending platforms.

E-commerce: The pandemic accelerated the adoption of e-commerce in Kuwait, creating opportunities for online retailers, logistics providers, and digital payment solutions.

Digital Infrastructure: Investments in digital infrastructure, including high-speed internet, data centers, and cybersecurity, are crucial to support the growth of the digital economy.

Renewable Energy and Sustainability:

Solar Energy: Kuwait has abundant sunshine, making it an ideal location for solar energy projects. Investments in solar power generation, solar panel manufacturing, and energy storage solutions hold significant potential.

Green Buildings and Infrastructure: As Kuwait seeks to reduce its carbon footprint, opportunities exist in green building construction, energy-efficient infrastructure development, and sustainable transportation solutions.

Waste Management and Recycling: Investing in modern waste management and recycling facilities can address environmental concerns and create a circular economy.

Tourism and Hospitality:

Luxury Tourism: Kuwait has the potential to attract high-end tourists with its rich cultural heritage, modern infrastructure, and proximity to other Gulf destinations. Investments in luxury hotels, resorts, and unique tourism experiences can cater to this segment.

Cultural and Heritage Tourism: Kuwait's historical sites, museums, and cultural events offer opportunities for investments in cultural and heritage tourism, including restoration projects, visitor centres, and cultural tours.

Business and MICE Tourism: Kuwait's role as a regional business hub can be further strengthened by investments in conference centres, exhibition facilities, and business hotels to attract MICE (Meetings, Incentives, Conferences, and Exhibitions) tourism.

Education and Training:

Private Education: The demand for high-quality education in Kuwait creates opportunities for investments in private schools, universities, and specialized training institutions.

Vocational Training: Expanding vocational training programs to meet the needs of a diversified economy presents opportunities for investments in technical schools, apprenticeship programs, and skills development centres.

Ed-Tech: The growing adoption of technology in education creates opportunities for investments in edtech platforms, online learning solutions, and educational software.

Healthcare:

Specialized Healthcare Services: Kuwait's growing population and increasing demand for specialized healthcare services create opportunities for investments in specialized hospitals, clinics, and diagnostic centres.

Medical Tourism: Kuwait can attract medical tourists from neighbouring countries by developing world-class healthcare facilities and offering competitive pricing.

Health-Tech: Investments in health-tech solutions, such as telemedicine platforms, electronic health records, and healthcare data analytics, can improve efficiency and access to healthcare.

Key Takeaways for Investors: Navigating the Kuwaiti Investment Landscape

Kuwait's economic transformation presents a unique opportunity for investors seeking growth and diversification. However, realizing this potential requires a nuanced understanding of the Kuwaiti investment landscape and a strategic approach that aligns with the country's long-term vision. Here are key takeaways for investors to consider:

Navigating the Regulatory Environment:

Understanding the Legal Framework: Kuwait has a comprehensive legal framework governing foreign investment, including laws related to company formation, foreign ownership, and repatriation of profits. Investors need to thoroughly research and understand these laws to ensure compliance and avoid potential pitfalls.

Obtaining Licenses and Permits: Depending on the sector and nature of the investment, investors may need to obtain various licenses and permits from different government agencies. This process can be complex and time-consuming, requiring careful planning and engagement with the relevant authorities.

Seeking Professional Guidance: Engaging legal and financial advisors with expertise in Kuwaiti regulations can streamline the process and ensure a smooth investment journey.

The Power of Local Partnerships:

Accessing Market Insights: Local partners can provide invaluable insights into market dynamics, consumer preferences, and competitive landscape, helping investors make informed decisions.

Navigating Cultural Nuances: Understanding and respecting Kuwaiti culture and business practices is crucial for building strong relationships and establishing trust. Local partners can act as cultural guides and facilitate effective communication.

Leveraging Networks and Connections: Local partners often have established networks and connections with key stakeholders, including government officials, business leaders, and potential customers, which can open doors for investors.

Embracing a Long-Term Vision:

Aligning with National Development Priorities: Kuwait's Vision 2035 outlines the country's long-term development goals, including economic diversification, human capital development, and sustainable growth. Investors who align their investments with these priorities are more likely to receive government support and contribute to the country's overall progress.

Patience and Persistence: Structural reforms and economic diversification take time to yield results. Investors need to be patient and persistent in their approach, recognizing that the full potential of the Kuwaiti market may not be realized immediately.

Building Sustainable Businesses: Investors should focus on building sustainable businesses that create value for the Kuwaiti economy, generate employment opportunities, and contribute to the long-term well-being of the country.

Managing Risks and Challenges:

Political Risks: Kuwait's political landscape can be complex, and investors need to be aware of potential political risks that could impact their investments. Staying informed about political developments and engaging with relevant stakeholders can help mitigate these risks.

Economic Volatility: As an oil-exporting country, Kuwait's economy is susceptible to fluctuations in global oil prices. Investors need to factor in this volatility and develop strategies to manage potential economic downturns.

Competition: Kuwait's market is becoming increasingly competitive, with both local and international players vying for opportunities. Investors need to develop a strong value proposition and a competitive edge to succeed.

Seizing the Opportunities:

First-Mover Advantage: Early investors in emerging sectors, such as renewable energy, technology, and tourism, can gain a first-mover advantage and establish a strong market presence.

Government Incentives: The Kuwaiti government offers various incentives to attract foreign investment, including tax breaks, subsidies, and access to financing. Investors should explore these incentives to maximize their returns.

Impact Investing: Investors seeking to make a positive social and environmental impact can find opportunities in Kuwait's growing focus on sustainability and social development.

In conclusion, investing in Kuwait requires a strategic and informed approach. By carefully navigating the regulatory environment, building strong local partnerships, embracing a long-term vision, and managing risks effectively, investors can capitalize on the country's vast potential and contribute to its economic transformation.

Chapter conclusion: Charting a Course for a Brighter Future

Kuwait stands at a crossroads. While its abundant oil wealth provides a cushion, the country must embrace comprehensive and well-sequenced reforms to navigate the changing global economic landscape. The IMF report offers valuable insights and recommendations for policymakers to chart a course towards a more diversified, dynamic, and sustainable economy, ensuring prosperity for current and future generations. The message is clear: Kuwait has the resources and potential to thrive in the post-oil era, but bold and decisive action is needed to unlock this potential.

Kuwait stands at a crossroads, poised between the comfort of its oil-driven past and the promise of a more diversified and sustainable future. The country's abundant wealth, derived from decades of oil dominance, has provided a comfortable cushion, but it has also created a dependence that poses significant challenges in a rapidly changing global landscape.

Kuwait must confront its structural weaknesses, unlock the potential of its human capital, and foster a dynamic private sector that can drive sustainable growth and create opportunities for its burgeoning young population.

For investors, Kuwait presents a unique opportunity. The country's economic transformation will create new avenues for investment in sectors like technology, renewable energy, tourism, education, and healthcare. However, navigating the Kuwaiti investment landscape requires a nuanced understanding of the regulatory environment, a commitment to building strong local partnerships, and a long-term perspective.

Kuwait's journey towards a diversified and sustainable economy is a story waiting to be written. By embracing the challenges and seizing the opportunities, Kuwait can create a brighter future for its citizens and become a model for successful economic transformation in the region.

Bahaa G. Arnouk

Egypt: Navigating Egypt's Economic Transformation: Challenges, Opportunities, and a Glimpse of Hope

Egypt's economy is at a crossroads, facing a mix of headwinds and tailwinds as it strives for a private-sector-led resurgence. While challenges like high inflation and regional instability persist, the government's commitment to its IMF-backed reform program is starting to yield positive results. In this chapter, I delve into the Egypt's economy, exploring the key challenges, emerging opportunities, and what it all means for investors seeking to navigate this dynamic market.

Egypt's economic landscape is undergoing a significant transformation, navigating a challenging period while striving for a private-sector-led resurgence. In this chapter, I am drawing insights from different sources including the International Monetary Fund's (IMF) July 2024 Staff Report for the Third Review under the Extended Fund Facility, offers a nuanced perspective on the challenges and opportunities in the Egyptian market.

Battling Headwinds, Seeking Stability

Egypt's recent economic performance has been subdued, with growth slowing to 2.7% in FY2023/24. This slowdown is a result of multiple converging factors:

Global Economic Slowdown: The global economy is facing a period of uncertainty and reduced growth, driven by factors like the war in Ukraine, persistent inflation in major economies, and tightening global financial conditions. This has negatively impacted Egypt's economy through reduced demand for exports, lower tourism revenues, and decreased foreign investment.

Regional Conflicts: The conflict in Gaza and Israel has had a particularly strong impact on Egypt. Disruptions in the Red Sea have significantly reduced Suez Canal receipts, a vital source of foreign currency earnings and government revenue. The conflict has also negatively affected tourism, further straining the economy.

Domestic Challenges: High inflation, reaching a peak of 38% in September 2023, has been a major concern. While it has gradually abated to 27.5% in June 2024, it continues to erode purchasing power, dampen consumer spending, and create uncertainty for businesses. Additionally, high nominal domestic borrowing costs, driven by the need to combat inflation, have constrained investment and economic activity.

Despite these significant headwinds, the IMF report highlights positive developments that offer a glimmer of hope:

Commitment to Reform Program: The Egyptian government has demonstrated a strong commitment to implementing the economic reform program agreed upon with the IMF. This commitment has been crucial in restoring a degree of confidence in the Egyptian market.

Exchange Rate Unification: The recent unification of the exchange rate, a key element of the reform program, has been instrumental in stabilizing the foreign exchange market. It has eliminated the parallel market premium, reduced speculation, and improved access to foreign currency for businesses. This has, in turn, helped attract foreign inflows and alleviate pressures on the Egyptian pound.

Monetary Policy Tightening: The CBE's decisive monetary policy tightening, including a series of interest rate hikes, has been crucial in curbing inflation and anchoring inflation expectations. While these measures have had a contractionary impact on the economy in the short term, they are necessary to bring inflation under control and create a more stable macroeconomic environment for sustainable growth in the medium to long term.

Increased Investor Confidence: The combination of exchange rate unification, monetary policy tightening, and the government's commitment to reforms has contributed to a notable increase in investor confidence. This has been reflected in increased demand for Egyptian pound-denominated assets, including Treasury securities, from both domestic and non-resident investors.

While challenges remain significant, these positive developments indicate that Egypt is taking steps in the right direction. Sustained commitment to the reform program and prudent macroeconomic management will be essential to navigate the current headwinds and pave the way for a more stable and prosperous economic future.

Fiscal Consolidation: A Balancing Act

Egypt is navigating a complex and challenging fiscal landscape, characterized by high public debt and substantial financing needs. The government's gross debt is projected to reach 96.4% of GDP in FY2024/25, reflecting the cumulative impact of past deficits, exchange rate depreciation, and rising interest costs. This high debt burden limits the government's fiscal space and increases its vulnerability to economic shocks.

To address these challenges, the government is pursuing a strategy of fiscal consolidation, aiming to reduce the debt-to-GDP ratio and create a more sustainable fiscal position. The centrepiece of this strategy is the target of achieving a primary surplus of 3.5% of GDP (excluding divestment proceeds) in FY2024/25. This ambitious target requires a delicate balancing act:

- **Debt Reduction**: Achieving a primary surplus is essential to stabilize and eventually reduce the debt-to-GDP ratio.

> This requires a combination of revenue-enhancing measures and expenditure restraint. However, aggressive fiscal consolidation can have a contractionary impact on the economy, potentially undermining growth and exacerbating social challenges.
>
> - **Maintaining Essential Social Spending**: Egypt faces high levels of poverty and inequality, and social spending plays a vital role in protecting vulnerable populations and promoting human capital development. The government is committed to safeguarding social spending, particularly on programs like Takaful and Karama, food subsidies, and health insurance. However, fiscal constraints limit the scope for expanding these programs or introducing new initiatives.

The government's fiscal consolidation strategy involves several key elements:

Revenue Mobilization: A key pillar of the strategy is to increase tax revenues to create more fiscal space for debt reduction and essential spending. This involves:

Comprehensive VAT Reform: The government plans to introduce amendments to the VAT law by November 2024, aiming to simplify the system, reduce exemptions, and improve its efficiency and progressivity. This reform is expected to generate a structural increase in VAT revenue of at least 1% of GDP on a 12-month basis.

Other Tax Measures: The government is also pursuing a range of other tax measures, including widening the tax base, implementing a new Income Tax Law, adopting a withholding tax on freezone sales to the domestic market, and strengthening tax administration.

Subsidy Reform: Reducing untargeted fuel subsidies is another crucial element of the fiscal consolidation strategy. The government has committed to gradually restoring fuel prices to cost-recovery levels by December 2025. This will free up resources for more targeted social support programs and reduce fiscal risks associated with the energy sector.

Debt Management: An active debt management strategy is being implemented to reduce gross financing needs and the overall debt burden. This involves:

Extending Debt Maturity: The government is gradually lengthening the maturity of domestic debt issuance through auctions, reducing rollover risks and interest rate sensitivity.

Debt Swaps: Agreements with pension funds and insurance funds to extend the maturity of existing debt are being explored to reduce near-term financing pressures.

Improved Public Investment Management: A new framework has been established to monitor and control overall public investment, including off-budget investment by SOEs, to ensure consistency with macroeconomic objectives and avoid excessive borrowing for capital projects.

The success of Egypt's fiscal consolidation strategy will depend on several factors:

Sustained Commitment to Reforms: Consistent implementation of revenue-enhancing measures and expenditure restraint will be crucial to achieve the targeted primary surplus and reduce the debt burden.

Economic Growth: Strong economic growth will be essential to generate higher tax revenues and make debt reduction more manageable. However, fiscal consolidation itself can have a dampening effect on growth in the short term.

Social Stability: The government must carefully manage the social impact of fiscal consolidation, ensuring that essential social spending is protected and that vulnerable populations are not disproportionately affected by subsidy reforms or other austerity measures.

External Environment: Favourable external conditions, including stable global commodity prices and strong investor sentiment, will be important to support Egypt's fiscal consolidation efforts.

Overall, Egypt's fiscal consolidation strategy represents a delicate balancing act between the need to reduce debt and the imperative to maintain essential social spending. The government's commitment to this strategy is commendable, but sustained effort and careful management of risks will be essential to achieve a more sustainable fiscal position and create the conditions for inclusive and sustainable growth.

Structural Reforms: Paving the Path to Sustainable Growth

While macroeconomic stabilization is a crucial first step, Egypt's long-term economic success hinges on implementing ambitious structural reforms. These reforms are essential to address deep-rooted challenges that have hampered private sector development, hindered productivity growth, and constrained Egypt's economic potential. The IMF report highlights several key areas where structural reforms are urgently needed:

Redefining the Role of the State:

Implementing the State Ownership Policy: The State Ownership Policy aims to reduce the state's dominant role in the economy, level the playing field for private businesses, and foster a more competitive market environment. This involves a multi-pronged approach:

Divestment of State-Owned Assets: The government is committed to divesting from non-strategic sectors, with a target of US$3.6 billion in dollar inflows from divestment in FY2024/25.

This will not only generate revenue for debt reduction but also attract private investment and expertise.

Strengthening Corporate Governance: Enhancing transparency and accountability in SOEs is crucial to improve their efficiency and performance. The government is working on legislation to establish a central unit in the Prime Minister's office to oversee SOE governance and facilitate divestment.

Enhancing Transparency: Greater transparency in SOE operations, including financial reporting and procurement activities, is essential to ensure fair competition and prevent favoritism. The government is taking steps to expand its SOE database and publish aggregate annual reports.

Creating a More Conducive Business Environment:

Streamlining Regulations: Egypt's complex and often burdensome regulatory environment has been a major obstacle to private sector growth. The government needs to streamline regulations, reduce red tape, and make it easier for businesses to start, operate, and expand.

Enhancing Trade Facilitation: Improving trade logistics, simplifying customs procedures, and reducing trade barriers are crucial to boost exports and attract foreign investment. The government is implementing a risk-based approach to customs clearance and introducing a "Green Lane" to expedite the release of low-risk cargo.

Strengthening the Competition Framework: A robust competition framework is essential to prevent anti-competitive practices, promote innovation, and ensure a level playing field for businesses. The government is working to strengthen the independence and enforcement powers of the Egyptian Competition Authority (ECA).

Fostering a More Resilient and Competitive Financial Sector:

Enhancing Governance in State-Owned Banks: State-owned banks dominate Egypt's financial sector, and improving their governance practices is crucial to ensure financial stability and promote efficient allocation of credit. The government is planning to commission an independent assessment of state banks' policies, procedures, and controls.

Promoting Competition: Increasing competition in the banking sector is essential to reduce borrowing costs for businesses and improve access to finance. This requires creating a level playing field for private banks and encouraging the entry of new players.

Ensuring Financial Stability: Maintaining a sound and stable financial system is crucial to support economic growth. This involves strengthening prudential regulations, enhancing risk management practices, and closely monitoring banks' exposure to public sector agencies.

Navigating a Complex Path: Egypt's structural reform agenda is ambitious and faces significant challenges. Political will, effective implementation, and consistent follow-through will be crucial to overcome vested interests and achieve meaningful progress.

A Cautious Outlook, but with a Glimmer of Hope: a cautious outlook for Egypt's economy, recognizing the significant external and domestic risks is recommended. Regional conflicts, a potential global slowdown, high inflation, and fiscal risks from contingent liabilities require careful management. However, the government's commitment to its reform program offers a glimmer of hope. The IMF report provides a valuable roadmap for navigating this complex landscape, but sustained commitment to reforms and prudent policies are essential for a durable recovery and a more prosperous future for Egypt.

Key Takeaways for Investors: Navigating Egypt's Evolving Landscape

The IMF report provides valuable insights for investors considering opportunities in Egypt. While the country is undergoing a significant transformation and offers potential for growth, a cautious and informed approach is essential. Here are key takeaways for investors:

Thorough Risk Assessment is Paramount:

Acknowledge the Complex Risk Profile: While Egypt's economic reform program is yielding positive results, the country continues to face significant risks:

Geopolitical Risks: Regional conflicts, particularly the conflict in Gaza and Israel, pose ongoing threats to stability, trade, and investment.

Inflationary Pressures: Despite recent moderation, inflation remains elevated, posing challenges for businesses and eroding purchasing power.

Fiscal Vulnerabilities: High public debt, significant financing needs, and potential contingent liabilities from SOEs create fiscal risks that could impact investor returns.

Conduct Comprehensive Due Diligence: Investors should conduct thorough due diligence, going beyond headline figures to understand the underlying risks and opportunities in specific sectors and projects. This includes assessing the potential impact of geopolitical events, inflation, exchange rate fluctuations, and regulatory changes on investment prospects.

Prioritize Investments Aligned with Sustainable Growth:

Focus on Private Sector-Led Growth: The IMF report emphasizes the importance of private sector-led growth as the engine for sustainable economic development. Investors should prioritize projects that contribute to private sector expansion, innovation, and job creation.

Support Economic Diversification: Reducing reliance on traditional sectors like tourism and energy and fostering growth in areas like manufacturing, technology, and renewable energy is crucial for Egypt's long-term economic resilience. Investors should seek opportunities that align with this diversification agenda.

Contribute to Sustainable Development: Investing in projects that promote environmental sustainability, social inclusion, and good governance practices will not only generate financial returns but also contribute to Egypt's overall development goals.

Navigate the Complex Regulatory Landscape:

Understand the Evolving Regulatory Framework: Egypt's regulatory environment can be complex and subject to change. Investors need to develop a deep understanding of the legal and regulatory framework governing their chosen sectors, including licensing requirements, tax policies, and labor laws.

Partner with Local Expertise: Navigating the intricacies of the Egyptian market can be challenging for foreign investors. Partnering with reputable local entities with strong expertise in legal, regulatory, and operational matters is crucial to mitigate risks and ensure compliance.

Engage with the Reform Agenda:

Advocate for Continued Reform Progress: The success of Egypt's economic transformation hinges on the government's sustained commitment to its reform agenda. Investors should actively engage with policymakers, industry associations, and other stakeholders to advocate for continued progress on reforms that improve the business environment, enhance transparency, and level the playing field.

Support Initiatives that Promote Good Governance: Investors can play a constructive role in promoting good governance practices by adhering to high ethical standards, supporting anti-corruption initiatives, and advocating for greater transparency and accountability in both the public and private sectors.

Monitor Macroeconomic Developments:

Stay Informed about Policy Changes: Egypt's macroeconomic situation is dynamic and subject to change. Investors should closely monitor developments related to inflation, exchange rate policy, fiscal balances, and debt management, as these factors can significantly impact investment returns.

Develop Contingency Plans: Given the uncertainties in the global and regional economic environment, investors should develop contingency plans to mitigate potential risks arising from adverse macroeconomic developments, such as sharp currency fluctuations, rising interest rates, or fiscal tightening.

Chapter conclusion: Charting a Course Through Turbulent Waters: A Path to Sustainable Growth?

Egypt's economic journey is undoubtedly fraught with challenges. The confluence of global headwinds, regional instability, and domestic pressures has created a complex and uncertain landscape. High inflation, a substantial debt burden, and the lingering effects of external shocks continue to weigh on the economy.

Yet, amidst these challenges, a glimmer of hope emerges. The Egyptian government's commitment to its IMF-backed reform program, as evidenced by the recent exchange rate unification and decisive monetary policy tightening, is starting to yield positive results. Investor confidence is gradually returning, financing conditions are improving, and inflation is showing signs of abating.

The road ahead remains long and arduous. Fiscal consolidation requires a delicate balancing act between debt reduction and maintaining essential social spending. Structural reforms, while crucial for unlocking Egypt's long-term growth potential, face significant implementation challenges. The success of mega-projects like Ras El-Hekma hinges on careful planning and risk management.

For investors, Egypt presents a mixed bag of opportunities and risks. Thorough risk assessment, a focus on sustainable investments aligned with the country's development goals, and a deep understanding of the evolving regulatory landscape are paramount. Active engagement with the reform agenda and close monitoring of macroeconomic developments are essential for navigating this dynamic market.

Ultimately, Egypt's economic future hinges on the government's ability to maintain its commitment to reforms, effectively manage risks, and create a more conducive environment for private sector-led growth. The IMF report provides a valuable roadmap, but the journey requires sustained effort, resilience, and a clear vision for a more prosperous and inclusive Egypt.

Bahaa G. Arnouk

Turkey:- Is Turkey the Emerging Market Comeback Story of 2025?

A nation undergoing a remarkable economic transformation. Following a period of significant challenges, decisive policy changes implemented in mid-2023 have paved the way for a return to macroeconomic stability and sustainable growth. This chapter explores and highlights the emerging opportunities for investors seeking resilient emerging markets.

Turkey's decisive shift in economic policies over the past year, as detailed in the International Monetary Fund's (IMF) October 2024 Article IV Consultation report, signals a robust commitment to macroeconomic stability and sustainable growth, presenting a compelling case for investors seeking resilient emerging markets.

From Crisis to Confidence: A Policy Turnaround

In 2023, Turkey found itself teetering on the brink of economic crisis. Inflation was rampant, exceeding 80 percent, fuelled by the CBRT's repeated cuts to policy rates in a misguided attempt to stimulate growth. This strategy backfired, triggering capital flight and a rapid depletion of the country's international reserves. By May 2023, the CBRT had haemorrhaged approximately US$30 billion in reserves since the start of the year, a stark indicator of the severity of the situation. The lira, under immense pressure, had depreciated by around 30 percent, further exacerbating inflationary pressures. To make matters worse, the Turkish government's response was to implement financial repression, including measures like interest rate caps on loans and forcing banks to hold government bonds at below-market rates. These actions, while intended to maintain a semblance of stability, only distorted the market, and ultimately worsened the economic imbalances.

However, a decisive policy shift initiated in mid-2023 marked a turning point. Recognizing the urgency of the situation, the newly elected government, in coordination with the CBRT, embarked on a comprehensive policy program aimed at restoring macroeconomic stability. The CBRT spearheaded this effort with a significant monetary tightening, aggressively hiking the policy rate from a mere 8.5 percent in May 2023 to a substantial 50 percent by March 2024. This bold move brought the real policy rate into positive territory for the first time in years, signalling a clear commitment to fighting inflation.

Simultaneously, the CBRT began dismantling the complex web of regulatory distortions that had been stifling the economy. They abolished interest rate caps on loans, removed the requirement for banks to hold government bonds at artificially low rates, and eliminated most of the other repressive measures that had been hindering market functionality. This decisive move towards financial liberalization, coupled with the aggressive monetary tightening, sent a powerful message to the markets that Turkey was serious about tackling its economic challenges.

Complementing the CBRT's actions, the government implemented fiscal measures designed to restore prudence and support the disinflation effort. These included increases in VAT rates, special consumption taxes on goods like petroleum and motor vehicles, and a hike in the corporate income tax (CIT) rate. While these measures were not without their challenges, they demonstrated the government's commitment to fiscal responsibility and its willingness to take tough decisions to stabilize the economy.

This comprehensive policy turnaround, characterized by a decisive shift towards orthodox economic policies, had a profound impact on market sentiment. Confidence in the Turkish economy began to revive, as evidenced by a sharp improvement in market indicators. Domestic and foreign investors, sensing a renewed commitment to stability, started shifting back into lira-denominated assets. Recognizing the positive changes, all major ratings agencies upgraded Turkey's sovereign risk ratings, further bolstering confidence in the country's economic prospects.

Taming Inflation: A Gradual but Steady Approach

Bringing inflation under control remains a top priority for Turkey. After reaching a peak of 75 percent in May 2024, inflation has begun to recede, falling to 52 percent in August 2024. This initial decline can be attributed to the lagged effects of the significant monetary tightening implemented by the CBRT, as well as the government's efforts to curb excessive wage growth and move towards a more contractionary fiscal stance.

The IMF report projects a further decline in inflation to 24 percent by the end of 2025, driven by a continuation of these policies. The CBRT remains committed to maintaining tight monetary policy, keeping the real policy rate in positive territory to dampen demand and anchor inflation expectations. The government, on its part, is pursuing a more disciplined fiscal approach, aiming to reduce the budget deficit and avoid policies that could reignite inflationary pressures. This includes a commitment to limit public sector wage increases and a more cautious approach to social spending.

However, the authorities are acutely aware of the risks associated with a rapid disinflation. A sudden and sharp decline in inflation could potentially destabilize the financial system, particularly given the high levels of dollarization in the economy. Additionally, a rapid tightening of fiscal policy could have adverse social consequences, especially for vulnerable households already struggling with the high cost of living.

Therefore, the Turkish authorities are pursuing a gradual and measured approach to taming inflation. This strategy, while taking longer to achieve the desired outcome, prioritizes a balanced approach that minimizes potential disruptions to financial stability and social well-being. The challenges associated with such gradual approach can be anticipated, highlighting the risk that shocks, such as commodity price volatility or escalating geopolitical tensions, could derail the disinflation process.

Despite these risks, the Turkish authorities remain steadfast in their commitment to this balanced strategy. They believe that a gradual approach, while requiring patience and careful management, offers the best path to achieving sustainable price stability without jeopardizing the hard-won gains in financial stability and social support. They are closely monitoring key economic indicators and are prepared to adjust their policies as needed to ensure that the disinflation process remains on track.

Growth Rebound: Anchored by Structural Reforms

While the necessary policy adjustments to combat inflation have led to a slowdown in economic growth in 2024, with GDP projected to expand by a modest 3 percent, the IMF anticipates a recovery to begin in early 2025. This recovery, projected to reach 2.7 percent in 2025 and eventually stabilize around a respectable 4 percent in the medium term, will be driven not just by the receding inflation but also by a series of ambitious structural reforms. These reforms, a crucial component of Turkey's economic strategy, are aimed at addressing long-standing challenges and unlocking the country's full growth potential.

At the heart of these reforms lies a focus on enhancing productivity. Recognizing that sustainable growth requires more than just favourable macroeconomic conditions, the Turkish government is implementing measures to improve the efficiency and competitiveness of the economy. This includes investments in education and skills development to equip the workforce with the knowledge and capabilities needed for a modern, knowledge-based economy. It also involves promoting innovation and technological adoption across various sectors, from manufacturing to agriculture, to boost output and create higher-value-added jobs.

Improving the business environment is another key pillar of the structural reform agenda. The government is committed to streamlining regulations, reducing bureaucratic hurdles, and strengthening the rule of law to create a more attractive environment for both domestic and foreign investment. This includes efforts to enhance transparency and accountability in the public sector, as well as measures to improve the efficiency of the judicial system. A more predictable and business-friendly environment is expected to attract much-needed capital and expertise, driving investment and job creation.

Furthermore, the government is committed to fostering a more inclusive and sustainable growth model. This involves addressing issues of income inequality and social exclusion, ensuring that the benefits of economic growth are shared more broadly across society. This includes initiatives to increase female labor force participation, reduce informality in the labor market, and improve access to quality education and healthcare for all citizens. Additionally, the government is prioritizing environmental sustainability, promoting investments in renewable energy and resource efficiency to create a greener and more resilient economy.

These structural reforms, while potentially requiring time to fully materialize, are laying the foundation for a more robust and sustainable growth trajectory for Turkey. By addressing deep-rooted structural bottlenecks and fostering a more competitive, inclusive, and environmentally responsible economy, these reforms are expected to not only accelerate the recovery but also ensure that the benefits of growth are shared more equitably and contribute to a more prosperous and sustainable future for all Turkish citizens.

Investment Opportunities: A Diversified Landscape

Turkey's economic transformation, driven by a commitment to stability and reform, is creating a fertile ground for investment across a diverse range of sectors. As the country emerges from its economic challenges, a new era of opportunity is dawning, attracting investors seeking growth in a dynamic and strategically located emerging market.

Manufacturing: A Hub for Modernization and Innovation.

Turkey boasts a well-established and diversified manufacturing sector, with a strong presence in industries such as automotive, textiles, and electronics. These sectors, while already significant contributors to the economy, are ripe for modernization and innovation, presenting attractive opportunities for investors seeking to capitalize on Turkey's industrial prowess.

Automotive: Turkey is a major automotive manufacturing hub, producing vehicles for global brands like Ford, Fiat, and Renault. The sector is undergoing a significant transformation, driven by the global shift towards electric and autonomous vehicles. This presents opportunities for investors in areas such as battery production, charging infrastructure, and advanced driver-assistance systems.

Textiles: Turkey has a long and rich history in textile production, renowned for its high-quality fabrics and craftsmanship. The sector is embracing new technologies and sustainable practices, creating opportunities for investors in areas such as advanced materials, digital printing, and circular fashion.

Electronics: Turkey's electronics industry is rapidly expanding, driven by growing domestic demand and the country's strategic location as a bridge between Europe and Asia. This presents opportunities for investors in areas such as semiconductor manufacturing, consumer electronics, and smart home technologies.

Tourism: Untapped Potential in a World-Renowned Destination.

Turkey is a global tourism powerhouse, attracting millions of visitors each year with its stunning natural beauty, rich cultural heritage, and vibrant cities. While already a major player in the global tourism market, Turkey has vast untapped potential, particularly in niche segments like cultural and sustainable tourism.

Cultural Tourism: Turkey is home to a wealth of historical and archaeological sites, from the ancient ruins of Ephesus to the iconic Hagia Sophia in Istanbul. The government is investing in the preservation and promotion of these sites, creating opportunities for investors in areas such as heritage tourism, archaeological tours, and cultural experiences.

Sustainable Tourism: Turkey's diverse landscapes, from its pristine coastline to its mountainous interior, offer immense potential for sustainable tourism development. This includes opportunities for investors in eco-lodges, nature reserves, and adventure tourism activities, catering to the growing demand for responsible and environmentally conscious travel experiences.

Infrastructure: Building the Foundations for Future Growth

Turkey is undertaking significant investments in infrastructure, recognizing its crucial role in supporting economic growth and enhancing connectivity. This creates a wealth of opportunities for construction and engineering firms, particularly in areas such as transportation, energy, and logistics.

Transportation: Turkey is expanding its network of highways, railways, and airports to improve connectivity and facilitate trade. This presents opportunities for investors in areas such as road construction, high-speed rail projects, and airport development.

Energy: Turkey is diversifying its energy mix, investing in renewable energy sources and upgrading its power grid. This presents opportunities for investors in areas such as solar and wind power plants, energy storage, and smart grid technologies.

Logistics: Turkey's strategic location at the crossroads of Europe and Asia makes it a natural logistics hub. The government is investing in the development of logistics centres, ports, and warehousing facilities, creating opportunities for investors in areas such as supply chain management, freight forwarding, and e-commerce fulfilment.

Renewable Energy: A Burgeoning Market for Clean Technologies

Turkey is committed to transitioning to a cleaner and more sustainable energy future, setting ambitious targets for increasing renewable energy capacity. This creates a burgeoning market for investors in solar, wind, and other clean technologies.

Solar Power: Turkey has abundant sunshine, making it an ideal location for solar power generation. The government is providing incentives for solar power development, creating opportunities for investors in areas such as solar panel manufacturing, solar farm construction, and distributed solar energy systems.

Wind Power: Turkey's wind resources are also significant, particularly along its Aegean and Mediterranean coastlines. The government is promoting wind power development, creating opportunities for investors in areas such as wind turbine manufacturing, wind farm construction, and offshore wind energy projects.

Other Clean Technologies: Turkey is also exploring other clean energy technologies, such as geothermal energy, biomass energy, and hydropower. This presents opportunities for investors in a wide range of clean energy solutions, contributing to Turkey's energy transition and a more sustainable future.

Digitalization: A Young and Tech-Savvy Population Driving Digital Growth

Turkey is experiencing a digital revolution, fuelled by a young, tech-savvy population and a rapidly growing digital economy. This presents a wealth of opportunities for investors in sectors such as fintech, e-commerce, and digital service providers, seeking to tap into a market with immense potential for growth and innovation.

Fintech: Turkey's fintech sector is booming, driven by a surge in demand for digital financial services, particularly among younger generations. This presents opportunities for investors in areas such as mobile payments, online lending, digital banking, and blockchain technologies. The government is supportive of fintech development, creating a regulatory environment conducive to innovation and growth.

E-commerce: Turkey's e-commerce market is expanding rapidly, fuelled by increasing internet penetration and the convenience of online shopping. This presents opportunities for investors in areas such as online marketplaces, e-commerce platforms, logistics and delivery services, and digital marketing. The growth of e-commerce is also driving demand for digital payment solutions and online security services.

Digital Service Providers: Turkey's digital service sector is also experiencing significant growth, driven by the increasing adoption of cloud computing, artificial intelligence, and big data analytics. This presents opportunities for investors in areas such as software development, IT consulting, data centres, and cybersecurity services. The government is promoting the development of a digital ecosystem, investing in digital infrastructure, and supporting the growth of tech startups.

In addition to these specific sectors, Turkey's digital transformation is creating a broader ecosystem of opportunity. The government's commitment to developing a central bank digital currency (CBDC) further highlights the country's embrace of digital innovation. This, coupled with the increasing availability of high-speed internet and the growing adoption of mobile technologies, is creating a fertile ground for digital entrepreneurship and investment.

For investors seeking to capitalize on the growth of the digital economy, Turkey offers a compelling proposition. The country's young and tech-savvy population, coupled with a supportive regulatory environment and a rapidly expanding digital ecosystem, creates a unique and attractive investment landscape.

Navigating the Investment Landscape: A Balanced Perspective

While Turkey's economic resurgence presents a compelling case for investment, it's essential to approach the landscape with a balanced perspective, acknowledging both the opportunities and the potential challenges. Investors should carefully consider the following factors:

Policy Continuity: The Cornerstone of Sustainable Growth

The sustainability of Turkey's current policy trajectory, characterized by a commitment to macroeconomic stability, fiscal discipline, and structural reforms, is paramount for maintaining investor confidence and attracting long-term investment. The decisive policy shift initiated in mid-2023 has been instrumental in restoring confidence and setting the stage for economic recovery. However, maintaining this momentum will require continued commitment from policymakers to stay the course, resisting pressures to revert to populist policies that could undermine the hard-won gains.

Investors should closely monitor the political landscape and assess the government's commitment to maintaining fiscal prudence, adhering to a tight monetary policy stance until inflation is firmly under control, and continuing the implementation of structural reforms. Any signs of policy reversals or a weakening of resolve could erode investor confidence and dampen economic prospects.

Geopolitical Risks: Navigating a Complex Regional Landscape

Turkey's strategic location at the crossroads of Europe, Asia, and the Middle East exposes it to a complex geopolitical landscape, with regional dynamics and external shocks potentially impacting investor sentiment and economic performance. The ongoing conflicts in neighbouring Syria and Iraq, as well as tensions in the Eastern Mediterranean, can create uncertainty and volatility, affecting trade, tourism, and investment flows.

Investors should carefully assess the geopolitical risks associated with investing in Turkey, considering the potential impact of regional conflicts, political instability, and security threats. Diversifying investments across different sectors and regions within Turkey can help mitigate these risks. Additionally, staying informed about geopolitical developments and engaging in thorough due diligence is crucial for making informed investment decisions.

Structural Reforms: Unlocking Long-Term Growth Potential

The pace and depth of structural reforms will be a key determinant of Turkey's long-term growth potential and its ability to compete in the global economy. While the government has embarked on an ambitious reform agenda, addressing issues such as productivity, labor market rigidity, and the business environment, the success of these reforms will depend on their effective implementation and the government's commitment to seeing them through.

Investors should closely monitor the progress of structural reforms, assessing the government's commitment to addressing key bottlenecks and creating a more competitive and dynamic economy. The pace of reform implementation, the effectiveness of new policies, and the government's ability to overcome vested interests will be crucial indicators of Turkey's long-term economic prospects. Other Considerations are:

Currency Volatility: The Turkish lira has experienced significant volatility in recent years, reflecting economic challenges and geopolitical uncertainties. Investors should consider hedging strategies to mitigate currency risk.

Regulatory Environment: While Turkey has made progress in improving its regulatory environment, challenges remain in areas such as transparency, predictability, and consistency. Investors should carefully assess the regulatory landscape and engage in thorough due diligence before making investment decisions.

ESG Factors: Environmental, social, and governance (ESG) factors are increasingly important considerations for investors. Turkey is making progress in areas such as renewable energy and social inclusion, but challenges remain in areas such as environmental protection and corporate governance. Investors should assess ESG risks and opportunities when making investment decisions.

A Prudent Approach to Investment

Investing in Turkey requires a prudent and well-informed approach, balancing the potential rewards with the inherent risks. Thorough due diligence, careful risk assessment, and a long-term perspective are essential for navigating the investment landscape and capitalizing on Turkey's economic resurgence.

By understanding the dynamics of the Turkish economy, the government's policy priorities, and the potential challenges and opportunities, investors can make informed decisions and contribute to Turkey's sustainable development while achieving their investment objectives.

Chapter conclusion: Is Turkey the Emerging Market Comeback Story of 2025?

Turkey is a nation undergoing a remarkable economic transformation. Following a period of significant challenges, decisive policy changes implemented in mid-2023 have paved the way for a return to macroeconomic stability and sustainable growth. This chapter explores the key findings of the report, highlighting the emerging opportunities for investors seeking resilient emerging markets.

Turkey's decisive shift in economic policies over the past year, as detailed in the International Monetary Fund's (IMF) October 2024 Article IV Consultation report, signals a robust commitment to macroeconomic stability and sustainable growth, presenting a compelling case for investors seeking resilient emerging markets. The report highlights a series of policy adjustments and structural reforms that have been instrumental in steering the Turkish economy away from the precipice of crisis and towards a path of sustainable growth.

The year 2023 was a turbulent one for Turkey, marked by soaring inflation, dwindling foreign currency reserves, and a widening current account deficit. The situation was exacerbated by a series of unorthodox economic policies that ultimately proved unsustainable. However, the newly elected government, recognizing the urgency of the situation, embarked on a bold and comprehensive policy program aimed at restoring macroeconomic stability.

At the heart of this turnaround was a decisive shift towards orthodox economic policies. The Central Bank of the Republic of Turkey (CBRT) implemented a significant monetary tightening, aggressively raising interest rates to curb inflation. This was accompanied by a move towards financial liberalization, dismantling the complex web of regulatory distortions that had been stifling the economy. The government, on its part, implemented fiscal measures designed to restore prudence and support the disinflation effort.

These decisive actions have yielded positive results. Inflation, while still high, has begun to recede, and market confidence has been restored. The IMF report projects a further decline in inflation and a gradual recovery in economic growth, underpinned by structural reforms aimed at enhancing productivity, improving the business environment, and fostering a more inclusive and sustainable growth model.

This economic transformation presents a compelling proposition for investors seeking growth in a dynamic emerging market. Turkey's well-established manufacturing sector, its world-renowned tourism industry, its ongoing investments in infrastructure, its commitment to renewable energy, and its rapidly growing digital economy offer a diverse range of investment opportunities.

However, navigating the investment landscape in Turkey requires a balanced perspective. Investors should carefully consider factors such as policy continuity, geopolitical risks, and the pace and depth of structural reforms. While the outlook is positive, challenges remain, and a prudent and well-informed approach is essential for success.

In conclusion, Turkey's economic narrative is shifting from crisis to confidence. While risks remain, the opportunities for investors are undeniable. Turkey's economic resurgence, driven by a young and dynamic population, a strategic location, and a renewed commitment to stability and reform, positions it as a compelling investment destination for those seeking growth in a rapidly evolving global landscape. The time for strategic investment in Turkey is now.

Cyprus: A Beacon of Resilience and Transformation in the Mediterranean

Cyprus's economy has consistently demonstrated resilience and adaptability in the face of numerous external shocks. This chapter, drawing upon insights from different sources including the International Monetary Fund (IMF) May 2024 Article IV Consultation report, offers a comprehensive analysis of the challenges and opportunities present in the Cypriot market.

Beyond Tourism: A Diversification Imperative

While the sun-kissed beaches and rich cultural heritage of Cyprus continue to attract tourists from around the globe, the island nation recognizes that over-reliance on tourism exposes it to external shocks and limits its long-term growth potential. Diversification is not just a desirable goal; it's an economic imperative for Cyprus.

The good news is that Cyprus is already making strides in broadening its economic base. The Information and Communications Technology (ICT) sector is experiencing rapid growth, fuelled by a burgeoning start-up ecosystem and government initiatives to promote digital skills and infrastructure. Financial services, a traditional strength of Cyprus, remain robust, with the banking sector boasting sizable capital and liquidity buffers. The professional services sector, encompassing legal, accounting, and consulting services, is also expanding, attracting international businesses seeking a strategic location within the European Union.

This diversification drive is reflected in the IMF's positive outlook for Cyprus. The organization projects stable growth of 2.6% in 2024, gradually rising to its estimated potential of 3% over the medium term. This growth trajectory is underpinned by several factors:

Robust Investment: Cyprus is witnessing strong investment activity, particularly in sectors aligned with the European Union Recovery and Resilience Plan (RRP). These investments are directed towards infrastructure upgrades, renewable energy projects, and digital transformation initiatives, laying the foundation for a more sustainable and competitive economy.

Structural Reforms: The government is committed to implementing structural reforms aimed at enhancing the business environment, improving the efficiency of the judicial system, and addressing skill mismatches in the labor market. These reforms are crucial for attracting foreign investment, fostering innovation, and boosting productivity.

EU RRP Inflows: Cyprus is set to benefit from significant financial support through the EU RRP. These funds are being channelled towards projects that promote green growth, digitalization, and economic resilience, providing a much-needed boost to the diversification efforts.

The shift away from a tourism-centric economy is not without its challenges. Cyprus needs to address issues such as a relatively high public sector wage bill, skill shortages in certain sectors, and the need for further progress in resolving legacy non-performing loans. However, the government's commitment to fiscal prudence, structural reforms, and strategic investments, coupled with the support of the EU, creates a favourable environment for sustained and diversified growth in Cyprus.

Strategic Investments: Fuelling Growth and Sustainability

Cyprus is not just diversifying its economy; it's doing so with a clear focus on sustainability and future-proofing its growth trajectory. The government has identified strategic investment as a key driver of this transformation, particularly in areas aligned with the European Union Recovery and Resilience Plan (RRP). This forward-looking approach opens up a wealth of opportunities for businesses and investors seeking to be part of a dynamic and sustainable economy.

Here's a closer look at the key areas of strategic investment in Cyprus:

Green Transition: A Race Towards Climate Neutrality

Cyprus has set its sights on achieving climate neutrality by 2050, a goal that requires a fundamental shift in its energy mix and infrastructure. The island nation is blessed with abundant sunshine, making it ideal for harnessing solar energy. Ambitious plans are underway to significantly increase the share of renewable energy sources in the electricity grid, with solar power taking center stage. Wind energy, particularly offshore wind farms, is also being explored as a viable option.

Beyond electricity generation, Cyprus is promoting energy efficiency across all sectors, from buildings to transportation. This involves retrofitting existing structures to reduce energy consumption, implementing stricter building codes for new constructions, and promoting electric vehicles and public transportation. Green infrastructure projects, such as smart grids, energy storage solutions, and sustainable water management systems, are also high on the agenda.

These ambitious green initiatives create a plethora of opportunities for businesses and investors. Companies specializing in renewable energy technologies, energy storage solutions, smart grids, sustainable construction materials, and energy-efficient building designs are well-positioned to capitalize on this growing market.

Digital Transformation: Embracing the Fourth Industrial Revolution

Cyprus recognizes that digital transformation is not just about adopting new technologies; it's about fundamentally changing how businesses operate, how citizens interact with government services, and how the economy functions as a whole. The government is actively promoting digitalization across all sectors, from healthcare and education to finance and tourism.

This involves investing in digital infrastructure, such as high-speed broadband networks and data centers, to ensure reliable and affordable connectivity for all. Efforts are underway to upskill the workforce, equipping citizens with the digital literacy and technical skills needed to thrive in a digital economy. The government is also streamlining regulations and processes to create a more business-friendly environment for digital entrepreneurs and investors.

This digital transformation wave presents lucrative opportunities for financial technology companies offering innovative payment solutions, digital banking services, and blockchain applications. Digital service providers specializing in e-commerce platforms, cloud computing, cybersecurity, and data analytics are also in high demand. The burgeoning field of Artificial Intelligence offers opportunities for companies developing AI-powered solutions for various sectors, from healthcare diagnostics to personalized education.

Infrastructure Development: Building for the Future

Cyprus is strategically investing in infrastructure projects that enhance energy security, improve connectivity, and support economic growth. Two flagship projects stand out:

Euroconnector Electricity Interconnector: This ambitious project aims to connect the electricity grids of Cyprus and Greece via an undersea cable, ending the island's energy isolation and enabling it to import electricity from the European mainland. This will not only enhance energy security but also facilitate the integration of renewable energy sources into the grid.

Liquified Natural Gas (LNG) Import Terminal: The construction of an LNG import terminal will diversify Cyprus's energy sources, reducing its reliance on oil and providing a cleaner alternative for power generation. The terminal will also serve as a strategic hub for supplying LNG to other countries in the region.

These large-scale infrastructure projects create significant opportunities for construction companies, engineering firms, equipment suppliers, and project management consultants. The ripple effects of these projects will extend to other sectors, such as logistics, transportation, and hospitality, creating a multiplier effect on the economy.

Cyprus's commitment to strategic investments in these key areas is a clear signal of its determination to build a more sustainable, resilient, and competitive economy.

Navigating the Fiscal Landscape: A Prudent Path to Sustainable Growth

The country has consistently maintained large primary surpluses, a testament to its commitment to fiscal responsibility. This disciplined approach has resulted in a rapidly declining public debt ratio, creating a more stable and sustainable foundation for future growth.

Sustaining Primary Surpluses: Building a Buffer for the Future

Cyprus's commitment to fiscal prudence is evident in its plan to sustain large primary surpluses until public debt falls comfortably below 60% of Gross Domestic Product (GDP). This target, while ambitious, is achievable given the government's track record of fiscal discipline.

Maintaining these surpluses serves several crucial purposes:

Debt Reduction: The primary surplus directly contributes to reducing the public debt burden, freeing up resources that can be directed towards other priorities, such as investment and social spending.

Fiscal Space: By reducing debt and building up fiscal buffers, Cyprus creates room to maneuver in the event of unforeseen economic shocks, such as a global recession or a natural disaster.

Long-Term Sustainability: A low debt-to-GDP ratio enhances long-term fiscal sustainability, ensuring that future generations are not burdened with excessive debt.

However, the government recognizes that sustaining primary surpluses requires a delicate balancing act. It needs to ensure that fiscal consolidation does not stifle economic growth or disproportionately impact vulnerable segments of society. This is where the next two elements of the fiscal strategy come into play.

Prioritizing Investment Spending: Investing in the Future

While fiscal consolidation is essential, Cyprus understands that strategic investment is equally crucial for long-term growth and prosperity. The government is prioritizing capital expenditures, particularly those aligned with the Recovery and Resilience Plan (RRP). This ensures that public funds are directed towards projects that yield the highest long-term returns, such as:

Infrastructure Upgrades: Investing in modern and efficient infrastructure, including transportation, energy, and digital networks, is essential for enhancing competitiveness, attracting foreign investment, and improving the quality of life for citizens.

Green Transition: Funding renewable energy projects, energy efficiency initiatives, and sustainable infrastructure is crucial for achieving Cyprus's ambitious climate goals and creating a more environmentally friendly economy.

Digital Transformation: Investing in digital infrastructure, skills development, and e-government initiatives is essential for unlocking the potential of the digital economy and creating new opportunities for businesses and citizens.

By prioritizing these strategic investments, Cyprus is not just spending money; it's investing in its future.

Implementing Structural Reforms: Creating a More Efficient and Competitive Economy

Fiscal prudence and strategic investment alone are not enough to guarantee sustainable growth. Cyprus recognizes the need for structural reforms to enhance the efficiency and competitiveness of its economy. Key areas of focus include:

Judicial Reform: Streamlining judicial processes, reducing backlogs, and improving the efficiency of the court system are crucial for strengthening the rule of law, attracting foreign investment, and creating a more predictable business environment.

Public Sector Efficiency: Enhancing the efficiency of the public sector, reducing bureaucracy, and improving service delivery are essential for reducing costs, improving citizen satisfaction, and freeing up resources for other priorities.

Labor Market Reforms: Addressing skill mismatches in the labor market, promoting lifelong learning, and attracting skilled foreign workers are crucial for meeting the needs of a diversifying economy and boosting productivity.

These structural reforms are not just about cutting costs or increasing efficiency; they're about creating a more dynamic, competitive, and inclusive economy that benefits all Cypriots.

Cyprus's fiscal strategy is a testament to its commitment to responsible and sustainable economic management. By sustaining primary surpluses, prioritizing strategic investment, and implementing structural reforms, the country is laying the groundwork for a brighter and more prosperous future.

A Stable and Attractive Investment Climate: A Gateway to Opportunity

Cyprus is not just an island of sun-drenched beaches and ancient ruins; it's a thriving hub for business and investment, offering a stable and welcoming environment for those seeking to expand their horizons. The country's strategic location, coupled with its EU membership and business-friendly policies, make it a compelling destination for foreign investors.

European Union Membership: A Foundation of Stability and Trust

Cyprus's accession to the European Union in 2004 marked a turning point in its economic development. As a full member of the EU, Cyprus benefits from:

Stable Regulatory Framework: The EU's comprehensive legal and regulatory framework provides a predictable and transparent environment for businesses, ensuring fair competition and protecting investor rights.

Access to the Single Market: EU membership grants businesses in Cyprus access to the world's largest single market, with over 500 million consumers. This opens up a vast market for goods, services, and investment, fostering cross-border trade and economic integration.

Free Movement of Capital and Labor: The free movement of capital within the EU allows for seamless cross-border investment and financial transactions, while the free movement of labor enables businesses to attract skilled workers from across the bloc.

Financial Stability: Cyprus benefits from the stability of the Eurozone, with the euro serving as its currency. This provides a shield against currency fluctuations and reduces transaction costs for businesses operating within the Eurozone.

EU membership provides a strong foundation of stability and trust for investors, assuring them that their investments are protected by a robust legal framework and a stable economic environment.

Business-Friendly Policies: Streamlining the Path to Success

Cyprus is committed to creating a business-friendly environment that fosters entrepreneurship, innovation, and investment. The government is actively pursuing policies aimed at:

Streamlining Regulations: Efforts are underway to simplify and modernize regulations, reducing bureaucratic hurdles and making it easier for businesses to start, operate, and grow.

Improving Judicial Efficiency: The IMF report highlights ongoing efforts to reform the judicial sector, addressing backlogs, streamlining procedures, and enhancing the efficiency of the court system. A more efficient judiciary is crucial for resolving disputes fairly and swiftly, instilling confidence in investors and businesses.

Enhancing Transparency and Accountability: Cyprus is committed to promoting transparency and accountability in government processes, reducing corruption, and ensuring a level playing field for all businesses.

Attracting Foreign Talent: Recognizing the importance of skilled labor for economic growth, Cyprus is implementing policies to attract and retain foreign talent, particularly in sectors facing skill shortages.

These business-friendly policies, coupled with a skilled workforce and a competitive tax regime, make Cyprus an increasingly attractive destination for foreign investment.

Strategic Location: A Bridge Between Continents

Cyprus's strategic location at the crossroads of Europe, Asia, and Africa is a significant asset for businesses seeking to expand their reach and tap into new markets. The island nation serves as a:

Gateway to Europe: As an EU member state, Cyprus provides a convenient entry point for businesses seeking to access the European market.

Hub for the Middle East and North Africa: Cyprus's close proximity to the Middle East and North Africa makes it an ideal base for businesses operating in these regions.

Link to Asia: Cyprus's historical ties and growing economic relations with Asia, particularly China and India, position it as a bridge between East and West.

This strategic location, combined with its well-developed transportation infrastructure, including modern ports and airports, makes Cyprus an efficient and cost-effective hub for international trade and investment.

Cyprus offers a compelling combination of stability, opportunity, and strategic advantage for foreign investors. Its EU membership, business-friendly policies, and prime location make it a gateway to a world of possibilities.

Opportunities Amidst Transformation: A Tapestry of Investment Potential

Cyprus is undergoing a dynamic transformation, driven by a commitment to diversification, sustainability, and innovation. This transformation presents a unique window of opportunity for investors seeking to capitalize on emerging trends and tap into a growing economy with a bright future. The IMF report highlights several key areas ripe for investment in Cyprus:

Renewable Energy: Harnessing the Power of the Mediterranean Sun

Cyprus is blessed with abundant sunshine, making it an ideal location for harnessing solar energy. The government has set ambitious targets for increasing the share of renewable energy sources in the electricity grid, aiming to reach one-third by 2030. This ambitious goal opens up a vast landscape of opportunities for businesses and investors in the renewable energy sector.

Solar Power: Cyprus has immense potential for solar energy development, both at the utility-scale and the rooftop level. Opportunities abound for companies specializing in solar panel manufacturing, installation, and maintenance, as well as the development of solar farms and community solar projects.

Wind Energy: While solar power is the frontrunner, Cyprus is also exploring the potential of wind energy, particularly offshore wind farms. Companies with expertise in wind turbine technology, offshore construction, and wind farm management can find promising opportunities in this emerging sector.

Energy Storage: As the share of intermittent renewable energy sources increases, energy storage becomes crucial for ensuring grid stability and reliability. This creates a growing market for battery storage technologies, pumped hydro storage, and other innovative energy storage solutions.

Smart Grids: Modernizing the electricity grid is essential for integrating renewable energy sources and improving grid efficiency. Companies specializing in smart grid technologies, grid management software, and advanced metering infrastructure can find opportunities in this evolving sector.

Cyprus's commitment to renewable energy is not just about reducing its carbon footprint; it's about creating a more sustainable and resilient energy future for the island nation.

Information and Communications Technology and Digital Services: Riding the Digital Wave

Cyprus is embracing the digital revolution, recognizing the transformative power of technology to drive economic growth, enhance competitiveness, and improve the quality of life for its citizens. The ICT sector is experiencing rapid growth, fuelled by a supportive government, a burgeoning start-up ecosystem, and a growing pool of skilled talent.

Software Development: Cyprus is becoming a hub for software development, attracting companies specializing in custom software solutions, mobile applications, and enterprise software. The availability of skilled programmers and a favourable business environment make it an attractive location for software development outsourcing.

Data Analytics: The increasing availability of data is creating a surge in demand for data analytics expertise. Companies specializing in data mining, predictive modelling, and business intelligence can find opportunities in various sectors, from finance and healthcare to tourism and retail.

Cybersecurity: As businesses and governments become increasingly reliant on digital technologies, cybersecurity is paramount. Cyprus is home to a growing number of cybersecurity firms offering a range of services, including threat detection, vulnerability assessment, and incident response.

Cloud Computing: The adoption of cloud computing is accelerating, providing businesses with flexible and scalable IT solutions. Cloud service providers offering infrastructure-as-a-service (IaaS), platform-as-a-service (PaaS), and software-as-a-service (SaaS) can tap into this growing market.

Cyprus's digital transformation is creating a vibrant and dynamic ICT sector, offering a wide range of opportunities for businesses and investors seeking to be part of the digital future.

Financial Services: A Solid Foundation for Growth

Cyprus has a long-standing reputation as a well-regulated and reputable financial centre. Its financial services sector, encompassing banking, insurance, investment funds, and other financial activities, is a key pillar of the economy. Despite the challenges posed by the global financial crisis and the need to address legacy non-performing loans, Cyprus's financial sector remains resilient and continues to offer opportunities for investors.

Banking: Cyprus's banking sector is well-capitalized and liquid, with strong regulatory oversight. Opportunities exist for foreign banks seeking to establish a presence in the EU, as well as for investors looking to participate in the consolidation of the domestic banking sector.

Investment Funds: Cyprus is a popular jurisdiction for establishing and managing investment funds, particularly for investors targeting the European market. Its favourable tax regime, EU membership, and experienced fund administrators make it an attractive location for fund managers and investors.

Insurance: Cyprus's insurance sector is growing, driven by demand for life insurance, health insurance, and property insurance. The country's stable economy, favourable tax regime, and EU membership make it an attractive location for insurance companies seeking to expand their operations. Opportunities exist for both domestic and international insurers, particularly in niche markets such as marine insurance and reinsurance.

Tourism and Hospitality: Embracing Sustainability and Niche Markets

While diversification is a key priority for Cyprus, tourism remains a vital sector, contributing significantly to the economy and employment. However, the tourism industry is evolving, with a growing emphasis on sustainability, authenticity, and niche markets. This presents both challenges and opportunities for investors in the tourism and hospitality sector.

Sustainable Tourism: Cyprus is committed to developing a more sustainable tourism industry, reducing its environmental impact and preserving its natural and cultural heritage. This creates opportunities for businesses offering eco-friendly accommodation, sustainable tourism activities, and responsible travel experiences.

Niche Markets: Cyprus is moving beyond mass tourism, focusing on attracting visitors interested in niche markets such as cultural tourism, agrotourism, medical tourism, and sports tourism. This presents opportunities for specialized tour operators, boutique hotels, and businesses catering to specific interests.

Enhancing the Quality of the Tourism Product: Cyprus is investing in upgrading its tourism infrastructure, improving the quality of accommodation, and developing new attractions and experiences. This creates opportunities for hotel developers, restaurant operators, and businesses offering unique and memorable tourism experiences.

By embracing sustainability, exploring niche markets, and enhancing the quality of its tourism product, Cyprus is positioning itself as a high-quality and competitive destination in the Mediterranean.

Key Takeaways for Investors: Navigating the Cypriot Landscape

Cyprus presents a compelling investment proposition, but success requires a strategic and informed approach. Here are key takeaways for investors seeking to capitalize on the opportunities in this dynamic market:

Strategic Alignment: Charting a Course for Long-Term Success

Align with Cyprus's Vision: Don't just chase short-term gains; focus on projects that align with Cyprus's long-term development goals. The government has clearly prioritized economic diversification, the green transition, and digital transformation. Investments in these areas are more likely to receive government support, benefit from favourable policies, and contribute to the country's sustainable development.

Identify Synergies: Look for opportunities where your investment can create synergies with existing industries and contribute to the broader economic ecosystem. For example, a renewable energy project could not only generate clean electricity but also create jobs in manufacturing, installation, and maintenance.

Think Beyond Profit: While financial returns are essential, consider the social and environmental impact of your investment. Cyprus is committed to sustainable development, and investors who embrace this ethos are more likely to gain public support and build lasting partnerships.

Due Diligence: Mitigating Risk and Maximizing Returns

Regulatory Landscape: Thoroughly research and understand the regulatory environment in Cyprus, including licensing requirements, environmental regulations, and tax laws. Engage with legal and financial advisors to ensure compliance and avoid potential pitfalls.

Risk Assessment: Conduct a comprehensive risk assessment, taking into account factors such as political stability, economic volatility, and potential changes in government policies. Identify potential risks and develop mitigation strategies.

Global Economic Shifts: Consider the impact of global economic trends on your investment. For example, rising interest rates, supply chain disruptions, and geopolitical tensions can affect project costs, profitability, and market demand.

Partnerships: Leveraging Local Expertise and Networks

Local Partners: Collaborating with local partners is crucial for navigating the Cypriot market. Local partners bring valuable expertise, established networks, and an understanding of the cultural nuances that can make or break a deal.

Joint Ventures: Consider forming joint ventures with Cypriot companies to leverage their local knowledge, access resources, and share risks.

Government Engagement: Engage with government agencies and industry associations to gain insights into investment opportunities, policies, and incentives.

Investing in Cyprus requires a strategic mindset, a commitment to due diligence, and a willingness to build strong partnerships. By taking a long-term view, understanding the local context, and embracing collaboration, investors can position themselves for success in this dynamic and promising market.

Chapter conclusion: Cyprus: A Mediterranean Oasis of Opportunity Beckons

Cyprus stands at a crossroads, poised to transform its economy into a model of resilience, sustainability, and innovation. The IMF's 2024 Article IV Consultation report underscores the island nation's remarkable progress in navigating economic headwinds, diversifying its economic base, and attracting strategic investments.

While tourism will always remain a vital part of Cyprus's identity, the country is actively cultivating a more diversified and resilient economic landscape. The burgeoning ICT sector, robust financial services industry, and expanding professional services are attracting international businesses and investors seeking a stable and welcoming environment within the European Union.

Cyprus's commitment to sustainability is evident in its ambitious green transition goals, with renewable energy taking center stage. The island is embracing the digital revolution, fostering a dynamic ICT sector and promoting digitalization across all facets of its economy. Strategic infrastructure projects, like the Euroconnector and the LNG import terminal, are enhancing energy security and regional connectivity.

The government's prudent fiscal management, characterized by consistent primary surpluses and a declining public debt ratio, has created a solid foundation for sustainable growth. Prioritizing strategic investments, particularly those aligned with the EU RRP, is ensuring that public funds are directed towards projects that yield the highest long-term returns. Structural reforms are further enhancing the business environment, improving judicial efficiency, and addressing labor market challenges.

Cyprus's strategic location at the crossroads of three continents, coupled with its EU membership and business-friendly policies, makes it an ideal gateway for businesses seeking to expand their global reach. The island offers a compelling combination of stability, opportunity, and strategic advantage for discerning investors.

However, success in Cyprus requires more than just capital; it demands a strategic mindset, a commitment to due diligence, and a willingness to forge strong partnerships. Investors who align their vision with Cyprus's long-term development goals, thoroughly assess potential risks, and collaborate with local partners will be best positioned to reap the rewards of this dynamic and promising market.

The message is clear: Cyprus is open for business, and the time to seize the momentum is now.

Iraq's Investment Landscape Beyond the Headlines, Sensing the Potential

Iraq's potential as a lucrative market for investment remains undeniable, but the narrative has evolved. While significant opportunities exist, a nuanced understanding of the current economic landscape is crucial for investors. This chapter, drawing insights from different sources including the International Monetary Fund's (IMF) April 2024 Article IV Consultation report, provides a clearer picture of the challenges and opportunities in the Iraqi market.

Reconstruction and Rehabilitation: A Multi-Billion Dollar Opportunity

The commitment to rebuilding Iraq remains strong. The government's focus on stability and social cohesion, driving significant spending on public services and infrastructure is noticeable. This creates a fertile ground for international businesses, particularly in construction, engineering, and related sectors. The report highlights the government's commitment to prioritizing high-impact projects, like the Grand Al-Faw Port and the Karbala Refinery, which present attractive opportunities. Here's a deeper dive into the specifics:

Scale of Investment: The IMF report projects that Iraq's capital expenditure will reach 7% of GDP in 2024. With a projected nominal GDP of 345.7 trillion Iraqi Dinars. This figure alone represents a significant opportunity for businesses involved in infrastructure development.

Focus on Infrastructure: the government's focus on "rehabilitating and recovering the educational system through additional infrastructures" and "upgrading critical infrastructure, including those related to information and communication technologies" is clear. This indicates a strong demand for construction and engineering expertise in these areas.

Electricity Sector Reform: The need for reforms in the electricity sector, which is currently inefficient and unreliable is paramount. This presents opportunities for businesses specializing in power generation, transmission, and distribution, as well as those involved in renewable energy projects. The IMF suggests that "gradually moving towards cost recovery in the electricity sector could yield additional savings," which could be achieved through investments in domestic energy capacity and improvements in tariff collection.

Housing and Urban Development: With a rapidly growing population and ongoing urbanization, the demand for housing and related infrastructure is high. Significant and efficient investments in various sectors, including housing, indicating potential opportunities for businesses involved in residential construction, urban planning, and development.

Transportation Networks: Upgrading critical infrastructure which likely includes transportation networks is critical. This suggests opportunities for businesses involved in road construction, railway development, and airport expansion.

The Iraqi government's commitment to reconstruction and rehabilitation, coupled with the projected scale of investment, makes this sector a multi-billion-dollar opportunity for international businesses. By focusing on projects aligned with the government's priorities and leveraging their expertise, businesses can play a vital role in rebuilding Iraq's infrastructure and contributing to its economic development.

Beyond Oil: Diversification and the Global Economy

While oil remains a key driver, potentially earning US$5 trillion in revenues between 2013-2035, Iraq is actively pursuing economic diversification. The need for structural reforms to unlock private sector-led growth is vital. This opens doors for businesses in sectors like agriculture, manufacturing, and services.

Here's a more detailed look at the diversification efforts and opportunities:

Urgent Need for Diversification: Iraq's heavy reliance on oil revenue and its vulnerability to oil price fluctuations is clear. The IMF staff consultation report states that "without additional diversification efforts, Iraq's external position is highly vulnerable to global energy transition risks." This underscores the urgency for Iraq to develop non-oil sectors to achieve sustainable economic growth.

Structural Reforms as Key Enablers: The report stresses that structural reforms are crucial for unlocking private sector-led growth and diversification. It specifically recommends:

Labor Market Reforms: levelling the playing field between public and private jobs, strengthening institutional capacity to ensure an adequate work environment and labor protection, and addressing impediments to female labor participation are paramount.

Business Environment Improvements: This involves fixing the inefficient and unreliable electricity sector, upgrading critical infrastructure, and accelerating WTO accession.

Governance and Anti-Corruption Measures: Enhance governance and prevent and combat corruption, including strengthening public procurement frameworks and business regulations is of critical importance and can't be ignored.

Sector-Specific Opportunities:

Agriculture: Iraq has significant agricultural potential, but the sector faces challenges related to water scarcity, outdated farming practices, and limited access to finance. Investment in modern irrigation techniques, improved crop varieties, and agricultural infrastructure can unlock the sector's potential.

Manufacturing: Developing a diversified manufacturing base can create jobs, reduce reliance on imports, and boost exports. Investment in light manufacturing, food processing, and building materials can be particularly promising.

Services: The services sector, including tourism, logistics, and financial services, has the potential to become a major driver of economic growth. Investment in infrastructure, skills development, and regulatory reforms can facilitate the growth of these sectors.

Global Initiatives and Synergies: China's Belt and Road Initiative (BRI): The report acknowledges the potential impact of the BRI on the region, including Iraq. The BRI's focus on infrastructure development, trade facilitation, and regional connectivity aligns with Iraq's diversification goals. Businesses can leverage the BRI to access funding, expertise, and market opportunities.

Other International Partnerships: Iraq can benefit from collaborations with other countries and international organizations to attract investment, transfer technology, and develop its non-oil sectors.

Iraq's economic future hinges on successful diversification. By implementing the recommended structural reforms and capitalizing on global initiatives, Iraq can create a more diversified and resilient economy, opening up a wealth of opportunities for businesses across various sectors.

Navigating the Fiscal Landscape: Balancing Act and Reform Drive

The IMF report paints a realistic picture of Iraq's fiscal landscape, acknowledging both the challenges and the government's proactive approach to addressing them. While fiscal pressures exist, it also recognizes the government's commitment to responsible fiscal management, which should instil confidence in potential investors. Here's a closer look at the details, challenges are:

Widening Deficit: The IMF report projects that Iraq's fiscal deficit will widen to 7.6% of GDP in 2024, driven by increased spending and declining oil prices. This poses a significant challenge to fiscal sustainability and highlights the need for corrective measures.

Rising Public Debt: The report projects that government debt will rise to over 86% of GDP by 2029 if no policy changes are implemented. This trajectory raises concerns about debt sustainability and potential risks to macroeconomic stability.

Large Public Wage Bill: The report identifies the large public wage bill as a key driver of fiscal pressure. Mandatory hiring policies and generous public sector compensation have contributed to a bloated public sector, straining government finances.

Declining Oil Prices: The IMF report assumes a decline in oil prices over the medium term, which will further reduce government revenue and exacerbate the fiscal challenges.

Favourable Investment Climate: A Land of Opportunity Awaits

Despite the challenges, Iraq presents a compelling case for investment, offering a favourable climate and a range of emerging opportunities for discerning businesses.

Here's a closer look at what makes Iraq an attractive investment destination:

Competitive Tax Regime: Iraq boasts competitive corporate and individual tax rates, making it an attractive location for businesses seeking to optimize their tax burden.

Potential for Further Improvement: The report mentions the potential for "payroll tax reform" and "review of customs duties," which could further enhance the tax environment for businesses. These reforms could include simplifying the tax code, reducing tax rates, and streamlining tax administration.

Attracting Foreign Investment: A competitive tax regime can be a key factor in attracting foreign investment, as it reduces the cost of doing business and increases profitability.

Attractive Investment Requirements: The government has implemented policies to streamline investment procedures and reduce bureaucratic hurdles.

Ease of Doing Business: Attractive capital and investment requirements, including incentives for foreign investors, make it easier for businesses to establish and operate in Iraq. These incentives could include tax breaks, subsidies, and streamlined licensing procedures.

Investor Confidence: A transparent and predictable investment framework can boost investor confidence and encourage long-term investment.

Untapped Potential: As a country rebuilding its economy and infrastructure, Iraq offers vast untapped potential across various sectors.

First-Mover Advantage: This presents a first-mover advantage for businesses willing to invest early and capitalize on the emerging opportunities. Early investors can establish a strong market presence, build brand recognition, and secure access to resources and talent.

Growth Potential: The reconstruction and development efforts are expected to drive significant economic growth in the coming years, creating a favourable environment for businesses to thrive.

In addition to these factors, Iraq's strategic location, its young and growing population, and its abundant natural resources further enhance its investment appeal. By taking a strategic approach and leveraging the government's commitment to reform, investors can position themselves for success in this dynamic and evolving market.

Opportunities Amidst Transition: Riding the Waves of Change

Specific sectors poised for growth and transformation can be easily identified, presenting lucrative opportunities for investors who understand the evolving landscape:

Digitalization: Iraq's digital landscape is rapidly evolving, driven by increasing internet penetration, a young and tech-savvy population, and the government's push towards digitalization. This presents a wealth of opportunities for businesses operating in the digital space.

Fintech Boom: The report highlights the government's push towards digital payments and financial inclusion. This creates a fertile ground for fintech companies offering innovative solutions:

Mobile Payments: Providing convenient and accessible payment solutions for a population with limited access to traditional banking services.

Digital Banking: Offering online banking services, including account opening, money transfers, and bill payments, to reach a wider customer base.

Online Lending: Facilitating access to credit for individuals and businesses through online platforms, leveraging alternative credit scoring models.

E-commerce and Digital Services: As internet penetration increases and the digital economy expands, opportunities abound for businesses providing:

E-commerce Platforms: Developing online marketplaces to connect buyers and sellers, facilitating the growth of online retail.

Digital Marketing Services: Helping businesses reach their target audience through online channels, including social media marketing, search engine optimization, and content marketing.

Online Entertainment: Providing streaming services, online gaming platforms, and other forms of digital entertainment to cater to the growing demand for online content.

Data Centres and IT Infrastructure: The growing demand for digital services requires robust and reliable IT infrastructure. This creates opportunities for businesses specializing in:

Data Centres: Building and operating data centers to provide secure and reliable data storage and processing services.

Cloud Computing: Offering cloud-based services, such as software-as-a-service (SaaS), platform-as-a-service (PaaS), and infrastructure-as-a-service (IaaS), to enable businesses to access computing resources on demand.

Cybersecurity: Protecting businesses and individuals from cyber threats, providing services such as network security, data encryption, and threat intelligence.

Renewable Energy: Iraq is embarking on a path towards decarbonization, aiming to reduce its reliance on fossil fuels and transition to a more sustainable energy mix. This presents significant opportunities for investors in the renewable energy sector.

Decarbonization Drive: The report underscores Iraq's commitment to a decarbonization pathway and its goal of reducing reliance on fossil fuels. This opens doors for investors in renewable energy technologies:

Solar Energy: Harnessing Iraq's abundant sunlight to generate electricity through solar photovoltaic (PV) systems and concentrated solar power (CSP) plants.

Wind Energy: Utilizing Iraq's wind resources to generate electricity through wind turbines, particularly in areas with high wind speeds.

Hydropower: Exploring the potential for hydropower generation from dams and rivers, particularly in the northern regions of Iraq.

Energy Efficiency Solutions: Improving energy efficiency is a key component of the decarbonization strategy. Businesses offering energy-efficient technologies and services can find a receptive market:

Smart Grids: Modernizing the electricity grid to improve efficiency, reliability, and integration of renewable energy sources.

Energy Audits: Assessing energy consumption patterns in buildings and industries to identify opportunities for efficiency improvements.

Building Retrofits: Upgrading existing buildings with energy-efficient technologies, such as insulation, lighting, and HVAC systems.

Green Finance and Investment: The transition to a low-carbon economy requires significant investment. Opportunities exist for:

Green Finance Institutions: Providing financing for renewable energy projects and sustainable infrastructure development.

Impact Investors: Investing in companies and projects that have a positive environmental and social impact.

By capitalizing on these emerging trends and aligning their investments with Iraq's long-term development goals, businesses can position themselves for success in this dynamic and evolving market. The digitalization and renewable energy sectors offer significant growth potential, and by embracing these opportunities, investors can contribute to Iraq's economic transformation while generating attractive returns.

Key Takeaways for Investors: A Roadmap for Success in Iraq

Investing in Iraq requires a strategic approach that considers both the opportunities and the challenges. The IMF report provides valuable insights to guide investors towards success in this dynamic market. Here are key takeaways to keep in mind:

Due Diligence: Navigate the Fiscal Landscape with Prudence

Oil Price Volatility: A decline in oil prices over the medium term could impact government revenue and spending. Investors should thoroughly assess the potential impact of oil price fluctuations on their projects, particularly those in sectors closely linked to government funding or oil revenue.

Fiscal Risks: Fiscal challenges, including a widening deficit and rising public debt should be considered. Investors should carefully analyze the government's fiscal policies and debt sustainability to understand the potential risks to their investments.

Project-Specific Analysis: Conduct thorough due diligence on specific projects, considering factors such as regulatory approvals, land acquisition, environmental impact, and social considerations.

Partnerships: Unlock Success Through Local Expertise

Navigating the Regulatory Environment: Collaborating with local partners who understand the intricacies of the Iraqi regulatory landscape can significantly streamline the investment process. Local partners can provide valuable guidance on legal requirements, licensing procedures, and compliance matters.

Leveraging Local Knowledge: Local partners bring in-depth knowledge of the market, cultural nuances, and business practices, which can be invaluable for foreign investors. They can facilitate market entry, identify potential customers and suppliers, and build relationships with key stakeholders.

Joint Ventures and Strategic Alliances: Forming joint ventures or strategic alliances with local companies can provide access to resources, distribution networks, and established market presence.

Long-Term Vision: Align Investments with Iraq's Development Goals

Economic Diversification: Economic diversification is necessary for Iraq's long-term sustainability. Investors should prioritize projects that contribute to the growth of non-oil sectors, such as agriculture, manufacturing, renewable energy, and services.

Private Sector Growth: There is a need for structural reforms to unlock private sector-led growth. Investors should focus on projects that support the development of a vibrant and competitive private sector, creating jobs and fostering economic growth.

Sustainable Development: Align investments with Iraq's sustainable development goals, considering environmental and social impact. Prioritize projects that promote clean energy, resource efficiency, and social inclusion.

By embracing these key takeaways, investors can navigate the complexities of the Iraqi market, mitigate risks, and capitalize on the vast opportunities for growth and development.

Chapter conclusion: Iraq: A Land of Opportunity or Fiscal Uncertainty?

This chapter has explored the evolving business landscape in Iraq, while fiscal challenges, including a widening deficit and rising public debt can't be ignored, significant potential for growth and diversification in the Iraqi economy is clear.

The government's commitment to reconstruction and rehabilitation, particularly in infrastructure, presents a multi-billion-dollar opportunity for international businesses. The push for diversification beyond oil, driven by structural reforms and global initiatives like the BRI, opens doors for businesses in sectors like agriculture, manufacturing, renewable energy, and services.

However, navigating this dynamic market requires a strategic approach. Investors must conduct thorough due diligence, considering fiscal risks and oil price volatility. Partnering with local experts can be invaluable for navigating the regulatory environment and leveraging local knowledge. Most importantly, investors should adopt a long-term vision, aligning their investments with Iraq's development goals of economic diversification, private sector growth, and sustainable development.

Iraq stands at a crossroads, balancing the weight of its fiscal challenges with the promise of a brighter future. For investors who can sense the potential, navigate the complexities, and embrace a long-term perspective, Iraq offers a unique opportunity to contribute to its economic transformation and reap the rewards of its growth.

Jordan: A Beacon of Resilience in a Turbulent Region

Jordan's economy has demonstrated remarkable resilience in the face of a series of external shocks, maintaining macro-stability and achieving moderate economic growth. This chapter, drawing insights from different sources including the International Monetary Fund's (IMF) January 2024 report, provides a comprehensive overview of the challenges and opportunities present in the Jordanian market.

Weathering the Storm: A Story of Economic Resilience

Despite facing a perfect storm of global and regional challenges, Jordan has demonstrated remarkable economic resilience. The COVID-19 pandemic, the war in Ukraine, and the recent conflict in Gaza and Israel sent shockwaves through the global economy, impacting Jordan on multiple fronts. Yet, the Kingdom has managed to navigate these turbulent times, emerging with its economy relatively intact. Several factors underpin Jordan's ability to weather these storms.

Sound Macroeconomic Policies: Jordan entered this tumultuous period with a foundation of prudent fiscal and monetary policies. These policies, implemented over time, focused on maintaining fiscal discipline, controlling debt levels, and ensuring a stable monetary environment. This proactive approach provided a crucial buffer against external shocks.

International Support: Jordan has consistently received substantial support from the international community. This support, both financial and technical, has been instrumental in mitigating the impact of regional instability and global crises. Donors and international financial institutions have played a critical role in bolstering Jordan's resilience, allowing the country to maintain essential services and pursue development goals.

Central Bank's Steady Hand: The Central Bank of Jordan (CBJ) has played a pivotal role in maintaining macroeconomic stability. Its adept monetary policy management, particularly in response to inflationary pressures stemming from global commodity price shocks, has been commendable. The CBJ's proactive measures helped curb inflation, bringing it down to manageable levels and ensuring price stability.

These factors have collectively enabled Jordan to achieve moderate economic growth, averaging 2-3 percent annually, despite the challenging circumstances. This sustained growth, while modest, signifies the effectiveness of Jordan's economic policies and its ability to adapt to external pressures.

However, it's crucial to acknowledge that challenges remain. The global economic landscape continues to be uncertain, and regional instability persists. Jordan will need to continue its commitment to sound macroeconomic management, structural reforms, and diversification of its economy to navigate future challenges effectively.

Addressing Challenges: A Focus on Jobs and Growth

Jordan's economic resilience is commendable, but it is not without its challenges. The country faces a complex web of interconnected issues that require sustained effort and strategic interventions.

The Urgency of Job Creation: Unemployment, particularly among youth and women, casts a long shadow over Jordan's economic outlook. While the economy has demonstrated resilience, the rate of growth has not been sufficient to generate enough jobs to absorb the growing workforce or significantly improve living standards. This persistent challenge risks social cohesion and demands urgent attention.

Prioritizing Inclusive Growth: Jordan's economic growth needs to be not only robust but also inclusive. This means ensuring that the benefits of growth are broadly shared across all segments of society, particularly among vulnerable groups. Addressing income inequality and promoting equal opportunities are crucial for achieving sustainable and equitable development.

The Burden of Public Debt: Although Jordan has managed to stabilize its public debt, it remains elevated. This high debt burden limits the government's fiscal space, constraining its ability to invest in critical areas such as education, healthcare, and infrastructure – all of which are essential for long-term growth and job creation.

Key Areas of Focus: A Roadmap for Reform

The IMF report outlines a multi-pronged reform agenda for Jordan, focusing on key areas crucial for achieving sustainable and inclusive growth:

Fiscal Consolidation: Paving the Path to Sustainability

Jordan is committed to a gradual but steady fiscal consolidation strategy aimed at reducing public debt while safeguarding essential social spending and creating fiscal space for crucial investments. This delicate balancing act involves a three-pronged approach:

Broadening the Tax Base: Reforms will focus on broadening the tax base to ensure a more equitable distribution of the tax burden and enhance revenue mobilization. This may include reviewing tax exemptions and incentives, improving tax administration, and exploring new revenue streams.

Enhancing Tax Compliance: Strengthening tax compliance is crucial for maximizing revenue collection. This involves measures to deter tax evasion, improve tax audit mechanisms, and leverage technology to enhance transparency and efficiency in tax administration.

Improving Public Expenditure Efficiency: Optimizing public spending is essential for achieving fiscal sustainability. This includes rationalizing current expenditures, improving public procurement processes, and enhancing the effectiveness of social safety net programs.

Financial Sector Resilience: Safeguarding Stability

Jordan's banking sector remains resilient, characterized by healthy capitalization levels and prudent risk management practices. However, maintaining this stability requires ongoing vigilance and proactive measures:

Preserving Monetary and Financial Stability: The Central Bank of Jordan (CBJ) will continue to play a pivotal role in maintaining price stability, managing inflation, and ensuring a stable financial environment conducive to investment and growth.

Safeguarding the Exchange Rate Peg: Maintaining the stability of Jordan's exchange rate peg remains a key objective. The CBJ will continue to employ appropriate monetary policy tools to manage exchange rate pressures and safeguard the country's external competitiveness.

Implementing Financial Sector Reforms: The CBJ is committed to implementing the recommendations of the 2023 IMF-World Bank Financial System Stability Assessment. This includes strengthening financial sector supervision, enhancing crisis preparedness, and promoting financial inclusion.

Improving Efficiency of Public Utilities: Ensuring Sustainability

Jordan's electricity and water sectors face significant financial and operational challenges that threaten their long-term sustainability. Addressing these issues is crucial for ensuring access to these essential services for citizens and businesses:

Tariff Adjustments: Gradual and transparent tariff adjustments are necessary to align prices with the cost-of-service provision and ensure the financial viability of the electricity and water sectors. Social protection measures will be crucial to mitigate the impact of tariff adjustments on vulnerable households.

Cost-Saving Measures: Implementing cost-saving measures within the utilities is essential for improving efficiency and reducing financial losses. This includes optimizing operational processes, reducing technical and non-technical losses, and exploring renewable energy sources to diversify the energy mix.

Enhanced Governance: Strengthening governance within the utilities is crucial for ensuring transparency, accountability, and efficient service delivery. This includes improving corporate governance practices, enhancing regulatory oversight, and promoting stakeholder engagement.

Accelerating Structural Reforms: Unlocking Growth Potential

Jordan recognizes that achieving its economic aspirations requires a fundamental shift towards a more competitive, private sector-driven growth model. The country's Economic Modernization Vision provides a roadmap for these transformative reforms:

Improving the Business Environment: Creating a more business-friendly environment is crucial for attracting investment, fostering entrepreneurship, and creating jobs. This involves streamlining regulations, reducing bureaucratic hurdles, and ensuring a level playing field for businesses of all sizes.

Attracting Higher Levels of Investment: Jordan aims to attract higher levels of both domestic and foreign direct investment to fuel economic growth and create employment opportunities. This requires showcasing investment opportunities, providing incentives for investors, and ensuring a predictable and transparent investment climate.

Introducing Labor Market Reforms: Reforms aimed at enhancing labor market flexibility are essential for creating more job opportunities, particularly for youth and women. This includes aligning education and training programs with market demands, promoting active labor market policies, and addressing skills mismatches.

Enhancing Governance: Strengthening governance across all sectors is paramount for fostering a culture of transparency, accountability, and efficiency. This includes promoting good governance practices, combating corruption, and ensuring the rule of law.

By focusing on these key areas, Jordan aims to create a more resilient, inclusive, and dynamic economy capable of providing greater opportunities for all its citizens. The road ahead will require steadfast commitment, effective implementation, and ongoing dialogue among all stakeholders.

Opportunities for Investment: A Land of Potential

Despite the economic headwinds, Jordan offers a compelling value proposition for investors seeking to capitalize on emerging market opportunities and contribute to the country's sustainable development. Several sectors stand out as particularly promising:

Tourism: Rediscovering Ancient Wonders

Jordan boasts a rich tapestry of historical and cultural treasures, from the iconic ruins of Petra to the breathtaking landscapes of

Wadi Rum. The country's tourism sector holds immense untapped potential, poised for a resurgence as regional stability improves and global travel recovers.

Untapped Potential: Jordan's tourism offerings extend far beyond its renowned historical sites. The country boasts diverse landscapes, including the Dead Sea, coral reefs in Aqaba, and nature reserves teeming with biodiversity. This diversity presents opportunities for developing niche tourism products such as eco-tourism, adventure tourism, and medical tourism.

Government Support: The Jordanian government recognizes tourism's economic significance and is committed to fostering its growth. Incentives for tourism investment, infrastructure development, and marketing campaigns aimed at attracting international visitors are creating a more favourable environment for tourism businesses to thrive.

Regional Cooperation: Jordan is actively engaged in regional initiatives to promote tourism and attract visitors from neighboring countries. These collaborations offer opportunities for cross-border tourism packages and joint marketing efforts, expanding the potential market reach for tourism operators.

Information and Communication Technology (ICT): A Digital Hub in the Making

Jordan has emerged as a regional leader in the ICT sector, driven by a young, tech-savvy population, government support, and a strategic location at the crossroads of continents.

Skilled Workforce: Jordan boasts a young and increasingly educated workforce, with a growing pool of skilled ICT professionals. The country has invested heavily in education and training programs to equip its workforce with the skills needed to succeed in the digital economy.

Supportive Regulatory Environment: The Jordanian government has implemented policies and regulations designed to foster innovation and attract investment in the ICT sector. Tax incentives streamlined business registration processes, and a supportive legal framework are creating a conducive environment for tech startups and established companies alike.

Growing Startup Ecosystem: Jordan has witnessed a surge in tech startups in recent years, fuelled by a vibrant entrepreneurial culture, access to funding opportunities, and government initiatives to support innovation. This burgeoning startup ecosystem presents opportunities for investors seeking to tap into the next generation of tech disruptors.

Renewable Energy: Harnessing the Power of the Sun and Wind

Jordan is blessed with abundant renewable energy resources, particularly solar and wind. Recognizing the need to diversify its energy mix and reduce its reliance on imported fossil fuels, the country has embarked on an ambitious transition towards renewable energy.

Favourable Feed-in Tariffs: Jordan has implemented attractive feed-in tariffs to incentivize investment in renewable energy projects. These tariffs provide long-term price guarantees for electricity generated from renewable sources, making investments in solar and wind projects commercially viable.

Public-Private Partnerships: The Jordanian government is actively seeking public-private partnerships to develop large-scale renewable energy projects. These partnerships leverage the expertise and financial resources of the private sector to accelerate the deployment of renewable energy technologies.

Energy Security and Sustainability: Investing in renewable energy in Jordan aligns with global sustainability goals and contributes to the country's energy security. By reducing its dependence on imported fossil fuels, Jordan can enhance its energy independence and reduce its carbon footprint.

Infrastructure: Building for the Future

Jordan faces significant infrastructure needs, particularly in the water, transportation, and energy sectors. Addressing these infrastructure gaps is crucial for unlocking economic growth, improving living standards, and enhancing the country's competitiveness.

Public-Private Partnerships: The Jordanian government recognizes the importance of leveraging private sector expertise and capital to address its infrastructure needs. Public-private partnerships (PPPs) are playing an increasingly important role in developing and financing large-scale infrastructure projects.

Water Security: Water scarcity is a pressing challenge in Jordan. Investment opportunities exist in water infrastructure projects such as desalination plants, wastewater treatment facilities, and water-efficient irrigation systems.

Transportation Networks: Modernizing Jordan's transportation networks is crucial for facilitating trade, reducing transportation costs, and connecting people to economic opportunities. Investment opportunities exist in road upgrades, railway expansion, and port development projects.

By embracing a forward-looking approach to economic development and actively seeking partnerships with the private sector, Jordan is positioning itself to overcome its challenges and capitalize on its unique strengths. For investors seeking to make a tangible impact while generating sustainable returns, Jordan offers a land of opportunity.

Key Takeaways for Investors: Navigating the Landscape

While Jordan presents compelling investment opportunities, a nuanced understanding of the country's operating environment and a strategic approach are essential for success. Here are key takeaways for investors to consider:

Due Diligence: A Foundation for Informed Decisions

Thorough due diligence is paramount before committing to any investment in Jordan. This involves a comprehensive assessment of the political, economic, and regulatory landscape, as well as the potential impact of regional dynamics on specific projects.

Political and Economic Risk Assessment: Understanding Jordan's political landscape, including government stability, policy direction, and regulatory frameworks, is crucial. Assessing economic indicators such as growth prospects, inflation, and currency stability provides further insights.

Regional Instability: Jordan's proximity to regions experiencing geopolitical tensions necessitates a careful evaluation of potential spillover effects. Investors should consider how regional instability might impact their investments and develop contingency plans to mitigate risks.

Sector-Specific Analysis: Conducting in-depth research on the specific sector of interest is essential. This includes understanding market dynamics, competitive landscape, regulatory environment, and potential challenges and opportunities within that sector.

Partnerships: Leveraging Local Expertise

Collaborating with local partners is highly advisable for navigating Jordan's business environment effectively. Local partners bring invaluable knowledge of the market, regulatory landscape, cultural nuances, and business networks.

Navigating Regulatory Complexities: Local partners can provide guidance on navigating Jordan's legal and regulatory frameworks, ensuring compliance with local laws and regulations, and facilitating necessary permits and approvals.

Accessing Networks and Relationships: Established local partners offer access to their existing networks and relationships, which can be invaluable for identifying opportunities, building trust, and resolving potential issues more effectively.

Cultural Understanding: Local partners provide insights into Jordan's cultural norms and business practices, facilitating smoother communication, building stronger relationships, and avoiding potential misunderstandings.

Long-Term Vision: Aligning with National Priorities

Investors should prioritize projects that align with Jordan's long-term development goals as outlined in the country's Economic Modernization Vision. Such alignment increases the likelihood of government support, facilitates a smoother investment process, and contributes to Jordan's sustainable development.

Economic Diversification: Projects that promote economic diversification by fostering growth in non-traditional sectors such as ICT, renewable energy, and tourism are particularly attractive.

Private Sector Growth: Investments that stimulate private sector growth, create jobs, and enhance competitiveness are highly valued. This includes supporting small and medium-sized enterprises (SMEs), which are considered the backbone of Jordan's economy.

Sustainability: Projects that prioritize environmental sustainability, social responsibility, and good governance practices align with Jordan's commitment to sustainable development and are more likely to receive favourable consideration.

By embracing a long-term perspective, conducting thorough due diligence, forging strong local partnerships, and aligning with Jordan's national priorities, investors can position themselves for success while contributing to the country's economic growth and sustainable development.

Chapter conclusion: Navigating Challenges, Seizing Opportunities

Jordan's economic journey is a testament to its resilience and adaptability. Despite facing a confluence of regional and global challenges, the Kingdom has managed to maintain macroeconomic stability and chart a course for sustained growth. This resilience is rooted in sound macroeconomic policies, unwavering international support, and the Central Bank of Jordan's adept monetary stewardship.

However, Jordan's path forward is not without its obstacles. Addressing persistent unemployment, particularly among youth and women, and ensuring inclusive growth that benefits all segments of society are paramount. The government's commitment to fiscal consolidation, structural reforms, and unlocking the potential of key sectors like tourism, ICT, and renewable energy will be crucial in navigating these challenges.

For investors, Jordan presents a compelling value proposition. The country's commitment to reform, coupled with its strategic location, young and skilled workforce, and untapped potential in key sectors, creates a fertile ground for investment. However, a nuanced understanding of the operating environment, thorough due diligence, and a long-term vision aligned with Jordan's national priorities are essential for success.

By embracing a collaborative approach, forging strong local partnerships, and capitalizing on the opportunities presented, investors can play a pivotal role in shaping Jordan's future. The Kingdom's journey towards sustainable and inclusive growth is a collective endeavour, one that requires the combined efforts of the government, private sector, and international community. By working together, we can help Jordan realize its full potential and emerge as a beacon of prosperity in the region.

Bahaa G. Arnouk

References

- IMF Country Report No. 24/280 on Saudi Arabia

- IMF Country Report No. 24/43 on Qatar

- IMF Country Report No. 24/31 on Oman

- IMF Country Report No. 23/223 on UAE

- IMF Country Report No. 23/331 on Kuwait

- IMF Country Report No. 24/274 on Egypt

- IMF Country Report No. 24/312 on Turkey

- IMF Country Report No. 24/137 on Cyprus

- IMF Country Report No. 24/128 on Iraq

- IMF Country Report No. 24/10 on Jordan